CW00739900

OLD ST. PAUL'S
CATHEDRAL

By

WILLIAM BENHAM, D.D., F.S.A.

Rector of St. Edmund the King, Lombard Street,
and Honorary Canon of Canterbury

LONDON

SEELEY AND CO. LIMITED, GREAT RUSSELL STREET

NEW YORK : THE MACMILLAN COMPANY

1902

LIST OF ILLUSTRATIONS

Wenceslaus Hollar—to whose engravings of Old St. Paul's we are indebted for our exceptional knowledge of the aspect of a building that has perished—was born in Prague in 1607, and was brought to England by the Earl of Arundel, who had seen some of his work at Cologne. He soon obtained profitable employment, producing engravings both of figures and views in rapid succession, and about 1639 he was appointed drawing-master to the Prince of Wales, afterwards Charles II. On the outbreak of the Civil War he served as a soldier in the Royalist ranks, and was taken prisoner at Basing House, but escaped to Antwerp. Obtaining very poor employment there, he returned to England in 1652, and was engaged upon the plates for Dugdale's *History of St. Paul's* and other works, for which, however, he is said by Vertue to have received very small pay, about fourpence an hour, "at his usual method by the hour-glass."

Some years later the Plague and the Fire again threw him out of employment, and he seems to have sunk deeper and deeper into poverty, dying in 1677, with an execution in his house, "of which he was sensible enough to desire only to die in his bed, and not to be removed till he was buried." He lies in the churchyard of St. Margaret's, Westminster, but there is no stone to his memory.

In the course of his industrious life he is said to have produced more than 2000 engravings and etchings. "He worked," says Redgrave, "with extraordinary minuteness of finish, yet with an almost playful freedom." His engravings of Old St. Paul's, though not entirely accurate, undoubtedly give a true general view of the Cathedral as it was in its last years, after the alterations and additions by Inigo Jones, and nearly a century after the fall of the spire.

OLD ST. PAUL'S

CHAPTER I.

THE BUILDING.

Roman London—The Beginning of Christian London—The English Conquest and London once more Heathen—The Conversion—Bishop Mellitus—King Sebert—The First Cathedral—Its Destruction—Foundation of the Second Cathedral by Bishop Maurice—Another Destructive Fire—Restoration and Architectural Changes—Bishop Fulk Basset's Restoration—The Addition Eastward—St. Gregory's Church on the S.W. side—" The New Work," and a New Spire: dedicated by Bishop Segrave—How the Money was raised—Dimensions of the Old Church—The Tower and Spire—The Rose Window at the East End—Beginning of Desecration.

THE Romans began the systematic conquest of Britain about the time of Herod Agrippa, whose death is recorded in Acts xii. London was probably a place of some importance in those days, though there is no mention of it in Cæsar's narrative, written some eighty years previously. Dr. Guest brought forward reasons for supposing that at the conquest the General Aulus Plautius chose London as a good spot on which to fortify himself, and that thus a military station was permanently founded on the site of the present cathedral, as being the highest ground. If so, we may call that the beginning of historic London, and the Romans, being still heathen, would, we may be sure, have a temple dedicated to the gods close by. Old tradition has it that the principal temple was dedicated to Diana, and it is no improbable guess that this deity was popular with the incomers, who found wide and well-stocked hunting grounds all round the neighbourhood. Ages afterwards, in the days of Edward III., were found, in the course of some exhumations, vast quantities of bones of cattle and stags' horns, which were assumed to be the remains of sacrifices to the goddess. So they may have

B

been ; we have no means of knowing. An altar to Diana was found in 1830 in Foster Lane, close by, which is now in the Guildhall Museum.

But not many years can have passed before Christianity had obtained a footing among the Roman people; we know not how. To use Dr. Martineau's expressive similitude, the Faith was blown over the world silently like thistle-seed, and as silently here and there it fell and took root. We know no more who were its first preachers in Rome than we do who they were in Britain. It was in Rome before St. Paul arrived in the city, for he had already written his Epistle to the Romans ; but evidently he made great impression on the Prætorian soldiers. And we may be sure that there were many " of this way " in the camp in London by the end of the first century. For the same reason we may take it for granted that there must have been a place of worship, especially as before the Romans left the country Christianity was established as the religion of the Empire. Only two churches of the Roman period in England can now be traced with certainty. Mr. St. John Hope and his fellow-explorers a few years ago unearthed one at Silchester, and the foundations of another may be seen in the churchyard of Lyminge in Kent.

And this is really all we can say about the Church in London during the Roman occupation. The story of King Lucius and that of the church of St. Peter in Cornhill are pure myths, without any sort of historical foundation, and so may be dismissed without more words.

The Romans went away in the beginning of the fifth century, and by the end of the same century the English conquest had been almost entirely accomplished. For awhile the new comers remained heathens ; then came Augustine and his brother monks, and began the conversion of the English people to Christ. The king of Kent was baptized in 596, and Canterbury became the mother church. Pope Gregory the Great sent Augustine a reinforcement of monks in 601. Two of these, Laurentius and Mellitus, were consecrated by Augustine as missionary bishops to convert West Kent and the East Saxon Kingdom to the faith. The chief town of the former district was Rochester, and of the latter London. This city had much grown in importance, having established a busy trade with the neighbouring states both by land and sea. The king of the East Saxons was Sebert, nephew of Ethelbert of Kent, and subject to him. He, therefore, received Mellitus with cordiality, and as soon as he established his work in the city, King Ethelbert built him a church wherein to hold his episcopal see, and, so it is said, endowed it with the manor of Tillingham, which is still the property of the Dean and Chapter of St. Paul's. There is no portion of that old church remaining. It was in all probability built mostly of wood, and it perished by fire, as so many Anglo-Saxon churches did, on July 7th, 1087. Some historical incidents connected with that early building will be found on a subsequent page.

In the year before this calamity (April 5th, 1086), Maurice, chaplain and chancellor to William the Conqueror, had been consecrated Bishop of London by Lanfranc. Unlike most of William's nominees to bishoprics, Maurice's moral character was disreputable; but he was a man of energy, and he set to work at once to rebuild his cathedral, and succeeded in getting from the king abundance of stone for the purpose, some of it from the remains of the Palatine tower by the side of the Fleet River, which was just being pulled down, having been hopelessly damaged by the fire,* and some direct from Caen. William also at the same time gave him the manor and castle of Bishop Stortford, thus making him a baronial noble. There was need for haste, for the Conqueror died at Rouen on the 9th of September that same year.

So began the great Cathedral of St. Paul, the finest in England in its time, which, witnessing heavy calamities, brilliant successes, scenes both glorious and sad, changes—some improvements and others debasements—lasted on for nearly six centuries, and then was destroyed in the Great Fire. We have first to note the main features of the architectural history.

Bishop Maurice began in the Norman style, as did all the cathedral-builders of that age, and splendid examples of their work are still to be seen in our cities. Bishop Maurice's, as I have said, was the finest of them all in its inception, but he really did little more than design it and lay the foundations, though he lived until 1108. He seems to have been too fond of his money. His successor, Richard Belmeis, exerted himself very heartily at the beginning of his episcopate,

---

* On the site of this old tower, Archbishop Kilwardby afterwards built the house of the Dominicans, or " Black Friars."

spent large sums on the cathedral, and cleared away an area of mean buildings in the churchyard, around which his predecessor had built a wall. In this work King Henry I. assisted him generously; gave him stone, and commanded that all material brought up the River Fleet for the cathedral should be free from toll; gave him moreover all the fish caught within the cathedral neighbourhood, and a tithe of all the venison taken in the County of Essex. These last boons may have arisen from the economical and abstemious life which the bishop lived, in order to devote his income to the cathedral building.

Belmeis also gave a site for St. Paul's School; but though he, like his predecessor, occupied the see for twenty years, he did not see the completion of the cathedral. He seems to have been embittered because he failed in attaining what his soul longed for— the removal of the Primatial chair from Canterbury to London. Anselm, not unreasonably, pronounced the attempt an audacious act of usurpation. Belmeis's health broke down. He was attacked with creeping paralysis, and sadly withdrew himself from active work, devoting himself to the foundation of the monastery of St. Osyth, in Essex. There, after lingering four years, he died, and there he lies buried.

King Henry I. died nearly at the same time, and as there was a contest for the throne ensuing on his death, so was there for the bishopric of London. In the interval, Henry de Blois, the famous Bishop of Winchester, was appointed to administer the affairs of St. Paul's, and almost immediately he had to deal with a calamity. Another great fire broke out at London Bridge in 1135, and did damage more or less all the way to St. Clement Danes. Matthew Paris speaks of St. Paul's as having been destroyed. This was certainly not the case, but serious injury was done, and the progress of the building was greatly delayed. Bishop Henry called on his people of Winchester to help in the rebuilding, putting forward the plea that though St. Paul was the great Apostle of the West, and had planted so many churches, this was the only cathedral dedicated to him. During these years Architecture was ever on the change, and, as was always the custom, the builders in any given case did not trouble themselves to follow the style in which a work had been begun, but went on with whatever was in use then.

Consequently the heavy Norman passed into Transitional, and Early

English. For heavy columns clustered pillars were substituted, and lancets for round arches. Nevertheless, apparently, Norman columns which remained firm were left alone, while pointed arches were placed over them in the triforium. Even in the Early English clustered pillars there were differences marking different dates, some of the time of the Transition (1222), and some thirty years later. And here let us note that the "Gothic" church, as it is shown in our illustrations, does not indicate that the Norman work had been replaced by it. The clustered pillars really encased the Norman, as they have done in other cathedrals similarly treated. At Winchester, William of Wykeham cut the massive Norman into Perpendicular order, but at St. Paul's an outer encasement covered the Norman, as Wren showed when he wrote his account of the ruined church. A steeple was erected in 1221. There was a great ceremony at the rededication, by Bishop Roger Niger, in 1240, the Archbishop of Canterbury and six other bishops assisting.

In 1255 it became necessary for the Bishop of London (Fulk Basset) to put forth appeals for the repair of the cathedral, and his ground of appeal was that the church had in time past been so shattered by tempests that the roof was dangerous. Some notes about these tempests will be found in a subsequent page. Accordingly this part was renewed, and at the same time the cathedral church was lengthened out eastward. There had been a parish church of St. Faith at the east end, which was now brought within the cathedral. The parishioners were not well content with this, so the east end of the crypt was allotted to them as their parish church, and they were also allowed to keep a detached tower with a peal of bells east of the church. This tower had already an historic interest, for it had pealed forth the summons to the Folkmote in early days, when that was held at the top of Cheapside. This eastward addition was known all through the after years as "The New Work." It is remarkable to note how much assistance came from outside. Hortatory letters were sent from the Archbishops of Canterbury and York, as well as from the greater number of other bishops, to their respective dioceses. And not only so, but eight Irish dioceses and one Scotch (Brechin) also sent aid.

There was another parish church hard by, that of St. Gregory-by-St. Paul. Almost all our cathedrals have churches close to them, such as

St. Margaret's, Westminster ; St. Laurence, Winchester ; St. John's, Peterborough ; St. Nicholas, Rochester. In all cases they are churches of the parishioners, as contrasted with those of the monastery or the cathedral body. St. Gregory's Church was not only near St. Paul's, but joined it ; its north wall was part of the south wall of the cathedral. Its early history is lost in antiquity, but it was in existence before the Conquest.* The body of St. Edmund, K. & M., had been preserved in it during the Danish invasions, before it was carried to Bury St. Edmunds by Cnut for burial. It shared the decay of the cathedral, and in the last days it was repaired, as was the west end, by Inigo Jones in his own style, as will be seen by the illustrations. Of the tombs and chantries which had by this time been set up, it will be more convenient to speak hereafter, as also of the deanery, which Dean Ralph de Diceto (d. 1283) built on its present site.

Before the end of the thirteenth century Old St. Paul's was complete. In the first quarter of the fourteenth century, a handsome marble pavement, "which cost 5d. a foot," was laid down over "the New Work," eastward, and the spire, which, being of lead over timber, was in a dangerous condition, was taken down and a very fine one set in its place, surmounted by a cross and a gilt pommel† large enough to contain ten bushels of corn. Bishop Gilbert Segrave (who had previously been precentor of the cathedral, and was bishop from 1313 to 1317) came to the dedication. "There was a great and solemn procession and relics of saints were placed within" (Dugdale). But the following extract from a chronicle in the Lambeth library is worth quoting : "On the tenth of the calends of June, 1314, Gilbert, Bishop of London, dedicated altars, namely, those of the Blessed Virgin Mary, of St. Thomas the Martyr, and of the Blessed Dunstan, in the new buildings of the Church of St. Paul, London. In the same year the cross and the ball, with great part of the campanile, of the Church of St. Paul were taken down because they were decayed and dangerous, and a new cross, with a ball well gilt, was erected ; and many

---

* Hence old Fuller's racy witticism : "S. Paul's is truly the mother church, having one babe in her body, S. Faith, and another in her arms, S. Gregory."

† A pommel was a ball made of metal, from Lat., *pomum :* "an apple." It was not uncommon to surmount church spires with hollow vessels and to take note of their capability of holding. Sometimes they were made in form of a ship, especially near ports where corn was imported.

A BISHOP PLACING RELICS IN AN ALTAR.

rom a Pontifical of the Fourteenth Century. British Museum, Laus. 451.

relics of divers saints were for the protection of the aforesaid campanile and of the whole structure beneath, placed within the cross, with a great procession, and with due solemnity, by Gilbert the bishop, on the fourth of the nones of October ; in order that the Omnipotent God and the glorious merits of His saints, whose relics are contained within the cross, might deign to protect it from all danger of storms. Of whose pity twenty-seven years and one hundred and fifty days of indulgence, at any time of the year, are granted to those who assist in completing the fabric of the aforesaid church."

In the Bodleian Library there is an inventory of these relics, amongst them part of the wood of the cross, a stone of the Holy Sepulchre, a stone from the spot of the Ascension, and some bones of the eleven thousand virgins of Cologne.

The high altar was renewed in 1309 under an indented covenant between Bishop Baldock and a citizen named Richard Pickerill. "A beautiful tablet was set thereon, variously adorned with many precious stones and enamelled work ; as also with divers images of metal ; which tablet stood betwixt two columns, within a frame of wood to cover it, richly set out with curious pictures, the charge whereof amounted to two hundred marks."

Dugdale also tells of " a picture of St. Paul, richly painted, and placed in a beautiful tabernacle of wood on the right hand of the high altar *in anno* 1398, the price of its workmanship amounting to 12*l*. 16*s*."

Quoting from a MS. of Matthew of Westminster, he gives the dimensions of the church, in the course of which he says the length was 690 feet. This is undoubtedly wrong, as Wren showed. I take the measurements from Mr. Gilbertson's admirable little handbook, who, with some modifications, has taken them from Longman's *Three Cathedrals.*

Breadth	104 ft.
Height of Nave roof to ridge of vaulting... ...	93 ft.
,, Choir	101 ft. 3 in.
,, Lady Chapel	98 ft. 6 in.
,, Tower from the ground	285 ft.
,, Spire from parapet of tower	204 ft.
,, Spire from the ground	489 ft.
Length of church (excluding Inigo Jones's porch)	586 ft.

Wren (*Parentalia*) thinks this estimate of the spire height too great ; he reckons it at 460 feet.

The cathedral resembled in general outline that of Salisbury, but it was a hundred feet longer, and the spire was sixty or eighty feet higher. The tower was open internally as far as the base of the spire, and was probably more beautiful both inside and out than that of any other English cathedral. The spire was a structure of timber covered with lead. In Mr. Longman's *Three Cathedrals* are some beautiful engravings after a series of drawings by Mr. E. B. Ferrey, reproducing the old building. There is one curious mistake : he has not given at the base of the spire, the corner pinnacles on the tower, which were certainly there. They are clearly shown in Wyngaerde's drawing of London, and on a seal of the Chapter, which we reproduce. Some time later than the rest of the work, stately flying buttresses were added to strengthen the tower walls. One special feature of the cathedral was the exquisite Rose window at the east end, of which we give an engraving. It had not a rival in England, perhaps one might say in Europe. Inigo Jones, if he was really the architect of St. Katharine Cree, made a poor copy of it for that church, where it may still be seen.

Of great historical events which had occurred during the growth of St. Paul's cathedral we have to speak hereafter. As the momentous changes of the sixteenth century drew near, the godlessness and unbelief which did so much to alienate many from the Church found strong illustrations in the worldliness which seemed to settle down awhile on St. Paul's and its services. Clergymen appeared here to be hired (Chaucer's *Prologue*), and lawyers met their clients. Falstaff "bought Bardolph at Paul's." But before we come to the great changes, it will be well to go back and take note of the surroundings of the cathedral, and also to stroll through the interior, seeing that we have now come to its completion as a building, except for one addition, a real but incongruous one, which belongs to the Stuart period. The accession of Henry VIII. then sees it, with that exception, finished, and we discern three main architectural features : there is still some heavy Norman work, some very excellent Early English, and some late Decorated. And there are also tombs of deep interest ; though they are not to be compared indeed with those of Westminster Abbey. There are only two Kings to whom we shall come in our walk. But let us have the outside first.

OLD ST. PAUL'S, FROM THE SOUTH. *After W. Hollar.*

CHAPTER II.

THE PRECINCTS.

The Cathedral Wall, its Course and Gates—Characteristic Names—The North Cloister—The Library—Pardon Churchyard—Minor Canons' College—Paul's Cross—Bishop's House—Lollards' Tower—Doctors Commons—The Cloister and Chapter House—The West Front.

A WALL was built round the churchyard in 1109, but was greatly strengthened in 1285. The churchyard had got such a bad character for robberies, fornications, even murders, that the Dean and Chapter requested King Edward I. to allow them to heighten this wall, with fitting gates and posterns, to be opened every morning and closed at night. From the north-east corner of Ave Maria Lane, it went east along Paternoster Row, to the end of Old Change, then south to Carter Lane, thence northwards to Creed Lane, with Ave Maria Lane on the other side. It will of course be remembered that the Fleet River ran along at the bottom of the hill, not bearing the best character in the world for savouriness even then, but crowded with boats as far as Holborn. It will be remembered that there was also a gate in the City Wall, on Ludgate Hill, a little to the west of St. Martin's Church. The gate had a little chapel within it, but the greater part of the building was used for a prison. Passing under it, and up Ludgate Hill, you came to the western gate of the Cathedral Close — a wide and strong one — spanning the street.* There were six of these gates; the second was at Paul's Alley, leading to the Postern Gate, or "Little North Door"; third, Canon's Alley; fourth, Little Gate (corner of Cheapside); fifth,

---

* In old times the name Ludgate Hill was given to that part which ran up from the Fleet to the City Gate. Inside the Gate the street was called "Bowyer Row," from the trade carried on in it. But it was also frequently called "Paul's." Ludgate was pulled down in 1760, and then Ludgate Hill became the name of the whole street.

St. Augustine's Gate (west end of Watling Street); and sixth, Paul's Chain. The ecclesiastical names bear their own explanation: "Ave Maria" and "Paternoster" indicated that rosaries and copies of the Lord's Prayer were sold in this street. "Creed" was a somewhat later name. In olden days, it was Spurrier's Lane, *i.e.*, where spurs were sold. But when an impetus was given to instruction under the Tudors, copies of the alphabet and the Creed were added to such articles of sale, and this was the place to get them. Paul's Chain got its name from the chain which was drawn across the gateway when service was going on, to prevent noise. The other names explain themselves.

Inside this area ran a cloister along the north side, turning a short distance southwards at the east end. This cloister was rebuilt by Dean More (1407—1421) round an enclosure which was a burial ground for clerics and men of mark in the City. The cloister was decorated by the series of paintings commonly known as the Dance of Death, such as may still be seen in the Cathedral of Basel, and in other places. Verses were appended to each picture, which were translated by Lydgate, the monk of Bury, and writer of poems on classical and religious subjects. Over the eastern side of the cloister was the library, a very fine one, but it perished in the Great Fire. The name "Pardon" applied to burial grounds, was not uncommon, apparently. The victims of the Black Death, in 1348, were buried in a piece of ground on the site of the Charter House, and this ground was known as Pardon Churchyard; and in the register books of St. Helen's, Bishopsgate, there are two entries of City magnates buried at different times by "the Pardon Door." Does it indicate that these particular burial grounds were bought with money paid for indulgences or expiations?

In the middle of the Pardon Churchyard of St. Paul's was a chapel of rich ornament, built by "Gilbert Becket, portgrave and principal magistrate in this City in the reign of King Stephen." He was the great Archbishop's father. The monuments in it and the surrounding churchyard are said to have rivalled in beauty those inside the cathedral. How this cloister and chapel fared, we shall see presently.

A FUNERAL PROCESSION.

From a MS. of the Hours of the Virgin. Fifteenth Century. British Museum, 27697.

North of the Pardon Churchyard was the College of the Minor, Canons, bordering on Paternoster Row ; and between it and the cathedral, in an open space, which in older times was the authorised meeting-place of the folkmote, was Paul's Cross.   There is no doubt of its exact situation, for during his valuable explorations into the history of the cathedral, Mr. Penrose discovered its foundations, six feet below the pavement, and this site is now marked by an inscription.   It is all now laid out as a pleasant garden, and a goodly number of people may be seen there daily feeding the tame pigeons.

I have shown already (see *Mediæval London*, p. 8) that the Folk-mote was held on a large green, east of the cathedral.   There were three such meetings yearly, to which the citizens were summoned by the ringing of the great cathedral bell.   When the first Cross was erected on the ground there is no record to show.   We may take for granted that there was first a pulpit of wood.   Not only were sermons preached, but proclamations and State announcements were delivered from it, also Papal bulls, excommunications, and the public penance of notorious offenders.   In the quaint language of Carlyle, Paul's Cross was "a kind of *Times* newspaper of the day."   On important occasions, the Lord Mayor and Aldermen came in state. Sometimes even the King came with his retinue, and a covered seat was placed for them against the cathedral wall, which may be noticed in our engraving.   If there was an important meeting, and the weather was unfavourable, the meeting was adjourned to the "Shrowdes," that is, to the crypt, which, as we have already seen, was now converted into the Church of St. Faith.

The Cross was damaged by lightning in 1382, and was rebuilt by Bishop Kempe (1448—1489).   It had stone steps, the pulpit was of strong oak, and it was roofed in with lead.   This was the building which was standing as we closed our account of the cathedral at the beginning of the Tudor dynasty.   We shall see more of it hereafter in our historical memorials.

On the north side of the Cathedral Nave was the Bishop's residence, with a private door leading into the cathedral.   Of the appearance of the west front of the cathedral we cannot speak with

CHAPTER III.

Fine coup d'œil *on entering the Nave—" Paul's Walk"—Monuments in Nave—*
Sir John Montacute—Bishop Kempe—Sir John Beauchamp, wrongly called
afterwards Duke Humphrey's—The Choir—Shrine of St. Erkenwald—Nowell
—Braybrooke—two Kings—many Bishops—Elizabethan Worthies.

THE aspect of the Nave, on entering the western door, must have
been magnificent. There were twelve bays to the nave, then the four
mighty pillars supporting the tower, then the screen closing in the
choir. The nave was known as " Paul's Walk," and not too
favourably known, either, under this title. Of this more hereafter.
At the second bay in the North Aisle was the meeting-place of
Convocation, closed in as a chamber. Here, too, was the Font, by
which was the Monument of Sir John Montacute. He was the son
of the first Earl of Salisbury, and it was his mother of whom the
fictitious story about the establishment of the Order of the Garter
by Edward III. was told. John de Montacute's father was buried
in the Church of the Whitefriars. The son was baptized in
St. Paul's, and directed in his will, " If I die in London I desire
that my body may be buried in St. Paul's, near to the font wherein
I was baptized."

At the sixth bay came "the Little North Door," and it was
answerable, as till lately was a similar door at St. Alban's Abbey, for
much of the desecration of the church which went on. There was
a notice on it that anybody bringing in burden or basket must pay a
penny into the box at hand. Between the columns of the tenth bay
was the Chantry of Bishop Kempe (1450—1489). It was the finest in
the cathedral, built by Royal licence. He did much for the
beautifying of the cathedral, and rebuilt Paul's Cross, as we have said
already. He seems to have kept clear of the fierce struggles

of the Wars of the Roses, for he saw rival kings in succession ostentatiously worshipping in St. Paul's, and did not lose the friendship of any of them. So far as one can judge, he honestly felt that he was not called upon to become a partisan of any, and this fact was recognised.

It was Edward IV. who gave him licence to erect his chantry. "For the singular reverence which he bore to God and to the blessed and glorious Virgin Mary, as also to the holy Apostles Peter and Paul, and to St. Erkenwald and Ethelbert, those devout confessors, he granted license to Thomas Kempe, Bishop of London, for the founding of a chantry of one priest, who should be the Bishop of London's confessor in this cathedral, for the time being, to celebrate divine service daily at the altar of the Holy Trinity in the body thereof, towards the north side, for the good estate of the said King and Queen Elizabeth, his Consort; as also of the said Bishop, during their lives in this world, and for the health of their souls after their departures hence, and moreover for the souls of the said King's progenitors; the parents and benefactors of the said bishop and all the faithful deceased; and to unite it to the office of confessor in this church for ever, and likewise to grant thereunto one messuage, one dovehouse, 140 acres of land, six acres of meadow, with eight acres of wood, called *Grays*, and 10s. rent with the appurtenances, lying in *Great Clacton* in the county of *Essex*; as also another messuage, twenty acres of land, two acres of meadow and two acres of wood, with the appurtenances in the same town, and two acres of land lying in *Chigwell*, together with the advowson of the Church of Chigwell, in the same county."

The next monument has a very strange and quaint interest. It was nearly opposite Kempe's, in the eleventh bay on the south side, that of Sir John Beauchamp, of Powick, in Worcestershire (son of Guy, Earl of Warwick), who died in 1374. He settled, out of some tenements in Aldermanbury, for the payment of 10 marks a year for a priest to celebrate at his altar, and 50s. a year for the special keeping of the anniversary of his death, December 3rd. There was a very fine image of the B.V.M. beside this tomb. Barnet, Bishop of Bath and Wells, gave a water mill, ninety acres of arable and pasture, and eight acres of wood, all lying at Navestock, in Essex, to the Dean and Chapter for the saying of certain prayers and a *de profundis* beside this image for the souls of the faithful; and there were constant oblations here. John Westyard, citizen and vintner, founded another altar at the same place for a chantry priest to say masses for the soul of Thomas Stowe, sometime Dean of St. Paul's, and for those of his parents and benefactors. In after years a strange mistake befell this tomb, one wonders why. It became popularly known as the tomb of Duke Humphrey, of whom we have more to say hereafter, who was buried not here but at St. Albans.

Entering within the choir, the first monument—a marble altar tomb —was that of Thomas Ewer, or Evere, who was Dean for twelve years, and died in 1400. In a straight line with it, before the steps of the high altar, lay Robert Fitzhugh, Bishop 1431—1436, who, as the learned Chancellor of the University of Cambridge, was sent as an English dele-gate to the Council of Basel. Whilst he was there he was elected to the See of London, and consecrated at Foligno. He was an earnest labourer for the betterment of the poor clergy in his diocese. Imme-diately behind the high altar screen was the magnificent shrine of St. Erkenwald, and beside it the tomb of Dean Nowell, both of which are described hereafter (see pp. 24, 51). East of this again, at the entrance to the Lady Chapel, was the beautiful brass of Robert Braybrooke, Bishop 1381—1405. His was a troublous time, the time of the evil government of Richard II. The Bishop exerted himself with all his might to bring about righteous government, and to draw the king away from evil counsellors. But he also persuaded the citizens to keep the peace when they would have run into riot, and was all his life held in honour. He was fierce against the Lollards, hardly to be wondered at, as they were constantly affixing papers against current doctrines and doings on the doors of the cathedral. It was this bishop who rebuked the citizens for their neglect of the Feast of the Conversion of St. Paul, their patron saint, and he made arrangements for special services, which from that time were carefully observed. He also gave directions for more devout observance of St. Erkenwald's Day, and set aside money from the See for the feeding of 15,000 poor people on that day in St. Paul's Churchyard. Robert Preston, a grocer, left a rich sapphire to the shrine, to be used for rubbing the eyes of persons who were threatened with blindness, and Braybrooke gave orders that the clergy should appear on all these high festivals in their copes, that nothing might be lacking to do them honour. He offered no opposition to the deposition of King Richard II. : it was clearly inevitable. Braybrooke was a vigorous reformer of abuses, and denounced the profanation of the church by traffickers, shooting at birds inside, and playing at ball.

Alongside the Lady Chapel, on the north side, was the chapel of St. George. We will now pass from it back by the north aisle. By the pillar north of the altar screen was the tomb of Sir Thomas Heneage. He was Vice-Chamberlain to Queen Elizabeth, and all his life was much trusted by her in matters of foreign diplomacy, though he sometimes got into trouble by taking too much on himself. His daughter Elizabeth was ancestress of the Earls of Winchelsea. He died in 1595.

Opposite this, at the North Wall, was the tomb of Ralph Hengham (d. 1311). Like so many great lawyers of old time he was in Holy Orders, Chancellor of the Diocese of Exeter, and also Chief Justice of the King's Bench. He was sent to the Tower for falsifying a document, which he is said to have done in order to reduce a fine imposed on a poor man from 13s. 4d. to 6s. 8d., and was himself fined heavily; the money being applied to building a clock tower in Palace Yard, opposite the door of Westminster Hall. Two judges, on being urged to tamper with records for beneficent purposes, are said to have declared that they did not mean to build clock towers! He was afterwards restored to office. He did good work in his day in compiling a Digest of the law.

SIR SIMON BURLEY, K.G., tutor and adviser of Richard II., beheaded on the charge of having corrupted the King's Court, 1388.

St. Paul's, as we see, was rich in tombs of mediæval bishops; as to Royalty it could not be named as compared with Westminster Abbey, for the City was not a royal residence except in very rare cases. But here we come to two tombs of Kings. Sebba was buried in the North Aisle in 695. He had been King of the East Saxons, but being afflicted with grievous sickness he became a monk. His tomb remained until the Great Fire, as did that of Ethelred the Unready, next to it. On the arches above were tablets containing the following inscriptions :—

"Hic jacet Sebba Rex Orientalium Saxonum ; qui conversus fuit

DOMVS CAPITVLARIS S. PAVLI a
Meridie Profpectus.

The Chapter House and Cloister. *After W. Hollar.*

THE NAVE, OR PAUL'S WALK. *After W. Hollar.*

THE CHOIR. *After W. Hollar.*

THE LADY CHAPEL. *After W. Hollar.*

THE ROSE WINDOW. *From the drawing by E. B. Ferrey in the Trophy Room, St. Paul's Cathedral.*

AREÆ ECCLESIÆ CATHEDRALIS S. PAVLI ICHNOGRAPHIA

Oriens

Septentrio

Meridies

NAVIS ECCLESIÆ

Scala Pedum.

EDOARDO DVSSÆEA.

a. Porticus
b. Ostium Occidentale
3. Turris
4. Cancellariæ Curia.
5. Ostium Septentri: minus
6. Ostium Merid: minus
7. Ostium Septentr: maius,
8. Ostium Merid: maius,
9. Capella Thomæ Kempe Lond: Episcopi.
10. Tumulus Ioh: Beauchamp,
11. Domus Capitularis
12. Gradus ad Chorum,
13. Ostium Chori,
14. Tumulus Ioh: Doune De-cani huius Eccl:
15. Mon: Ioh: Colleti, Decani huius Eccl:
16. Mon: Gulielmi Herel: Arm huius Eccl:
17. Mon: Gulielmi Cokayn Eq: Aur:

18. Mon: Nicholas Bacon Eq: aur. magni Sig: Angliæ custodis.
19. Tumulus Ioh: Nevecout
20. Tum: Valentini Greer
21. Tum: Bartholomæi de Oukly
22. Tum: Willelmi Byrbva,
23. Tum: Simonis Eadulph,
24. Tum: Ric: Lichfield,
25. Tum: Ioh: Actou.
26. Mon: Christophori Hattoni Ord Gart: Militis.
27. Tumu: Eustac: de Fauconberg Episc

28. Tum: Henr: de Wengham, Lon: Episc:
29. Tum: Henrici Lacie Com: Lincolniæ
30. Tum: Rob: de Braybroke Ep: Lon:
31. Tum: S. Erkenwaldi
32. Mon: Alexandri Nowell: Deca-ni huius Ecclesiæ
33. Mon: Vicecomi Hunerege Epi: Aur:
34. Tum: Rob: de Hergham
35. Tum: Sim: Burley Ord Gart: Mi:
36. Mon: Ioh: Gunlaviensis Lanc: Ducie
37. Man: Willielmi Herbert Com: Pembr:
38. Tum: Ioh: Heliæ
39. Tum: Ioh: de Chishull Lon: Ep:
40. Tum: Rob: Kyrri Lond: Ep:
41. Mon: Ioh: Maioris Equ: Au:
42. Mon: Gulielmi Aubrey.
43. Tum: Sebæ Sax: Regis.
44. Tum: Ethelredi Sax: Regis.
45. Tum: Thomæ de Evere.

46. Tum: Willielmi Greene
47. Tum: Rᵢ Filij Iluconis Ep: Lond:
48. Summum Altare,
49. Capella S. Georgij
50. Capella S. Dunstani

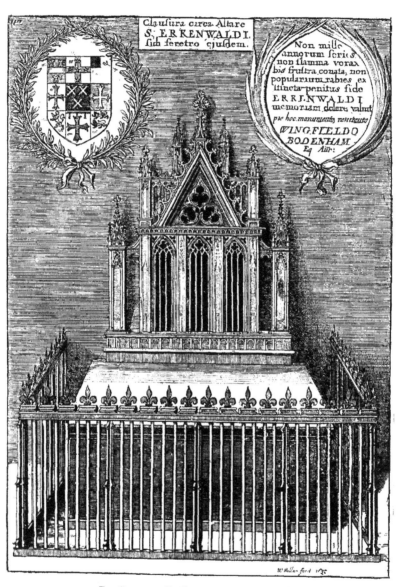

Claufura circa Altare
S. ERKENWALDI.
fub feretro ejufdem.

Non mille
annorum series
non flamma vorax
bis frustra conata, non
popularium rabies ex
stincta penitus fide
ERKENWALDI
memoriam delere valuit
pie hoc monumento restituente
WINGFIELDO
BODENHAM.
Eq Aur:

W. Hollar fecit 1655

THE SHRINE OF ST. ERKENWALD. *After W. Hollar.*

TOMBS OF SEBBA AND ETHELRED.   *After W. Hollar.*

ad fidem per Erkenwaldum Londonensem Episcopum, anno Christi
DCLXXVII. Vir multum Deo devotus, actibus religiosis, crebris precibus
& piis elemosynarum fructibus plurimum intentus ; vitam privatam &
Monasticam cunctis Regni divitiis & honoribus præferens : Qui cum
regnasset annos XXX. habitum religiosum accepit per benedictionem
Waltheri Londinensis Antistitis, qui præfato Erkenwaldo successit.
De quo Venerabilis Beda in historia gentis Anglorum."*

"Hic jacet Ethelredus Anglorum Rex, filius Edgari Regis ; cui in
die consecrationis hic, post impositam Coronam, fertur S. Dunstanus
Archiepiscopus dira prædixisse his verbis : Quoniam aspirasti ad regnum
per mortem fratris tui, in cujus sanguinem conspiraverunt Angli, cum
ignominiosa matre tua ; non deficiet gladius de domo tua, sæviens in te
omnibus diebus vitæ tuæ ; interficiens de semine tuo quousque Regnum
tuum transferatur in Regnum alienum, cujus ritum et linguam Gens
cui præsides non novit ; nec expiabitur nisi longa vindicta peccatum
tuum, & peccatum matris tuæ, & peccatum virorum qui interfuere
consilio illius nequam : Quæ sicut a viro sancto prædicta evenerunt ;
nam Ethelredus variis præliis per Suanum Danorum Regem filiumque
suum Canutum fatigatus et fugatus, ac tandem Londoni arcta obsidione
conclusus, misere diem obiit Anno Dominicæ Incarnationis MXVII. post-
quam annis XXXVI. in magna tribulatione regnasset."†

* "Here lieth Sebba, King of the East Saxons, who was converted to the faith by
Erkenwald, Bishop of London, in the year of Christ 677. A man much devoted to God,
greatly occupied in religious acts, frequent prayers, and pious fruits of almsgiving, preferring
a private and monastic life to all the riches and honours of the kingdom, who, when he had
reigned 30 years, received the religious habit at the hands of Walther, Bishop of London,
who succeeded the aforesaid Erkenwald, of whom the Venerable Bede makes mention in
his History of the English People."

† "Here lieth Ethelred, King of the English, son of King Edgar, to whom, on the day
of his hallowing, St. Dunstan, the archbishop, after placing the crown upon him, is said to
have foretold terrible things in these words : Forasmuch as thou hast aspired to the Kingdom
through the death of thy brother, against whom the English have conspired along with thy
wretched mother, the sword shall not depart from thy house, raging against thee all the days
of thy life, destroying thy seed until the day when thy Kingdom shall be conveyed to
another Kingdom whose customs and language the race over whom thou rulest knoweth not;
nor shall there be expiation save by long-continued penalty of the sin of thyself, of thy
mother, and of those men who took part in that shameful deed. Which things came to pass
even as that holy man foretold ; for Ethelred being worn out and put to flight in many
battles by Sweyn, King of the Danes, and his son Cnut, and at last, closely besieged in
London, died miserably in the year of the Incarnation 1017, after a reign of 36 years of
great tribulation."

c

Certainly in this latter terrible epitaph, it cannot be said that the maxim *de mortuis* was observed. But it speaks the truth.

Of a much later date is a royal monument, not indeed of a king, but of the son and father of kings, namely, John of Gaunt. He died in 1399, and his tomb in St. Paul's was as magnificent as those of his father in the Confessor's Chapel at Westminster, and of his son at Canterbury. It was indeed a Chantry founded by Henry IV. to the memory of his father and mother, Gaunt and Blanche of Lancaster. She was Gaunt's first wife (d. 1369), and bore him not only Henry IV., but Philippa, who became wife of the King of Portugal, and Elizabeth, wife of John Holland, Earl of Huntingdon. It was through Blanche that Gaunt got his dukedom of Lancaster. She died of plague in 1369, during his absence in the French Wars, and was buried here. Before his return to England he had married (in 1371) Constance, daughter of Pedro the Cruel, and hereby laid claim to the crown of Castile, as the inscription on his monument recorded. Their daughter married Henry, Prince of the Asturias, afterwards King of Castile. Constance died in 1394, and was also buried in St. Paul's, though her effigy was not on the tomb. In January, 1396, he married Catharine Swynford, who had already borne him children, afterwards legitimised. One of them was the great Cardinal Beaufort; another, John Beaufort, Earl of Somerset, was the grandfather of Margaret Tudor, mother of Henry VII. Gaunt's third wife (d. 1403) is buried at Lincoln. The long inscription on the monument closed with the words, " Illustrissimus hic princeps Johannes cognomento Plantagenet, Rex Castilliæ et Legionis, Dux Lancastriæ, Comes Richmondiæ, Leicestriæ, Lincolniæ et Derbiæ, locum tenens Aquitaniæ, magnus Seneschallus Angliæ, obiit anno xxii. regni regis Ricardi secundi, annoque Domini mcccxcix."

Close by John of Gaunt, between the pillars of the 6th bay of the Choir, was the tomb of WILLIAM HERBERT (1501—1569), first Earl of Pembroke of the second creation, a harum-scarum youth, who settled down into a clever politician, and was high in favour with Henry VIII., who made him an executor of his will, and nominated him one of the Council of twelve for Edward VI. He went through the reign of Mary not without suspicion of disloyalty, but was allowed to hold his place at Court, and in the reign of Queen Elizabeth he was accused of favouring the Queen of Scots, though here also he overcame the suspicions, and did not lose his place. He married Anne, the sister of Queen Catherine Parr, and they were both buried in St. Paul's.

JOHN OF CHISHULL, who filled the see from 1274—1280, and was Edward III.'s Chancellor, held a great number of valuable posts together. This may have produced the mental incapacity into which he fell. Archbishop Peckham had to appoint a commission to manage the diocese. He was buried against the wall of the North Aisle, not far from John of Gaunt.

ROGER NIGER, bishop from 1228 to 1241, was buried under the fifth bay of the Choir, between it and the North Aisle. There were three inscriptions on his tomb, the first on the aisle side:

"Ecclesiæ quondam Præsul præsentis, in anno
M bis C quater X jacet hic Rogerus humatus:
Hujus erat manibus Domino locus iste dicatus:
Christe, suis precibus veniam des; tolle reatus."

Then we have a short biography in laudatory terms, and below that a record which one may translate as it stands: "It came to pass while this Bishop Roger stood mitred [infulatus] before the high altar, ready to begin the Divine mysteries, there came on such a dense cloud that men could scarcely discern one another; and presently a fearful clap of thunder followed, and such a blaze of lightning and intolerable smell, that all who stood by fled hastily, expecting nothing less than death. The Bishop and one deacon only bravely remained, and when the air was at length purified the Bishop completed the service." We shall have more about this storm hereafter.

SIR JOHN MASON (1503—1566), the son of a cowherd at Abingdon, and afterwards a great benefactor to that town. His mother was a sister to the Abbot of Abingdon, and through this relationship he was educated at Oxford, became a Fellow of All Souls', took orders, and, in consequence of the skill which he displayed in diplomacy and international law, received rich Church preferments, among them the Deanery of Winchester. At the accession of Queen Mary he had to relinquish this, but as he had been faithful to her, she showed him much favour, and gave him some secular offices. On the accession of Elizabeth, he returned to his Deanery, and was all his life one of the most trusted of the Queen's councillors, especially in foreign matters.

DR. WILLIAM AUBREY was appointed Vicar-General of Canterbury by Archbishop Grindal, and was esteemed a great lawyer in his time. He was the grandfather of the famous antiquary (d. 1595).

Crossing the Choir, and beginning from the west, we will now proceed eastward along the South Aisle of the Choir. First, we come to two famous Deans, Donne and Colet, the account of whom belongs to a subsequent page. In fact, the greater number of monuments in this aisle are of later date than the others, but it will be more convenient to take them here, excepting those which are connected with the subsequent history. The wall monument of WILLIAM HEWIT (arms, a fesse engrailed between three owls) had a recumbent figure of him in a layman's gown. He died in 1599.

SIR WILLIAM COKAYNE (d. 1626) was a very rich Lord Mayor; high in the confidence of James I., who constantly consulted him on business. He was a munificent contributor to good works. It was said of him that "his spreading boughs gave shelter to some of the goodliest families in England." From his daughters descended the Earls of Nottingham, Pomfret, Holderness, Mulgrave, and Dover; the Duke of Ancaster, and the Viscounts Fanshawe.

JOHN NEWCOURT, Dean of Auckland, Canon of St. Paul's, Doctor of Law (d. 1485).

The handsome brass of ROGER BRABAZON, Canon of St. Paul's (d. 1498), had a figure in a cope. At the foot was the scroll, "Nunc Christe, te petimus, miserere quæsumus : Qui venisti redimere perditos, noli damnare redemptos"

Passing into the south side of the Lady Chapel, we come to two more mediæval Bishops of London : HENRY WENGHAM (1259—1262). He was Chancellor to Henry III. Close to him was EUSTACE FAUCONBRIDGE, a Royal Justiciary, and afterwards High Treasurer, and Bishop of London, 1221—1228.

WILLIAM RYTHYN, LL.D., was Rector of St. Faith's and Minor Canon of the Cathedral (d. 1400).

RICHARD LYCHFIELD, Archdeacon both of Middlesex and of Bath, Canon Residentiary of St. Paul's (d. 1496).

The tomb of SIR NICHOLAS BACON (1509—1579), Queen Elizabeth's famous minister, and father of the great philosopher, had his recumbent figure, and those of his two wives, Jane, daughter of William Fernley, and Ann, daughter of Sir Anthony Cooke. The latter was the mother of Francis. The Latin inscription on the tomb was most laudatory, and reads as if it came from the same pen that wrote the dedication of the *Advancement of Learning*.

Another of the Elizabethan worthies is SIR FRANCIS WALSINGHAM (d. April 6th, 1590). The monument to him was placed on the wall, with a long Latin biographical inscription and twenty lines of English verse.

Two other wall tablets in the same chapel commemorated other heroes of that period. SIR PHILIP SIDNEY, who died of his wound at Arnhem, October 15th, 1586, was buried in St. Paul's, with signs of public grief almost unparalleled. " It was accounted sin for months afterwards for any gentleman to appear in London streets in gay apparel." The tablet to him was of wood, and bore the following inscription :—

> " England, Netherlands, the Heavens and the Arts,
>   The Soldiers, and the World, have made six parts
>   Of noble Sidney ; for none will suppose
>   That a small heap of stones can Sidney enclose.
>   His body hath England, for she it bred,
>   Netherlands his blood, in her defence shed,
>   The Heavens have his soul, the Arts have his fame,
>   All soldiers the grief, the World his good name."

Close to this, on the same pillar, was a tablet to SIR THOMAS BASKERVILLE, who had also done good service as a brave soldier, according to the account given in fourteen lines of verse, which, it must be said, are a great deal more musical than Sidney's.

SIR CHRISTOPHER HATTON (1540—1591) had a finer monument than any of the other Elizabethan celebrities. Whether he deserved it is another matter. He was clever and handsome, and got into special favour with the Queen by his graceful dancing. He even wrote her

CHAPTER IV.

The First Cathedral—Mellitus and his Troubles—Erkenwald—Theodred "the Good" —William the Norman, his Epitaph—The Second Cathedral—Lanfranc and Anselm hold Councils in it—Bishop Foliot and Dean Diceto—FitzOsbert—King John's Evil Reign, his Vassalage—Henry III.'s Weak and Mischievous Reign —The Cardinal Legate in St. Paul's—Bishop Roger "the Black"—The three Edwards, Importance of the Cathedral in their Times—Alderman Sely's Irregularity—Wyclif at St. Paul's—Time of the Wars of the Roses—Marriage of Prince Arthur.

I HAVE already said that the buildings of the ancient cathedral, with a special exception to be considered hereafter, were completed before the great ecclesiastical changes of the sixteenth century.

Our next subject will be some history of the events which the cathedral witnessed from time to time during its existence, and for this we have to go back to the very beginning, to the first simple building, whatever it was, in which the first bishop, Mellitus, began his ministry. He founded the church in 604, and he had troubled times. The sons of his patron, King Sebert, relapsed into paganism, indeed they had never forsaken it, though so long as their father lived they had abstained from heathen rites. One day, entering the church, they saw the bishop celebrating the Sacrament, and said, " Give us some of that white bread which you gave our father." Mellitus replied that they could not receive it before they were baptized ; whereupon they furiously exclaimed that he should not stay among them. In terror he fled abroad, as did Justus from Rochester, and as Laurence would have done from Canterbury, had he not received a Divine warning. Kent soon returned to the faith which it had abandoned ; but Essex for a while remained heathen, and when Mellitus wished to return they refused him, and he succeeded Laurence at Canterbury. Other bishops ministered to the Christians as well as they could ; but the authority of the See and the services of the cathedral were restored by Erkenwald, one of the noblest of English prelates, son of Offa, King of East Anglia. He founded the two great monasteries of Chertsey and Barking, ruled the first himself, and set his sister Ethelburga over the other. In 675 he was taken from his abbey and consecrated fourth Bishop of London by Archbishop Theodore, and held the See until 693. He was a man, by universal consent, of saintly life and vast energy. He left his mark by strengthening the city wall and building the gate, which is called after him Bishopsgate. Close by is the church which bears the name of his sister, St. Ethelburga. He converted King Sebba to the faith; but it was probably because of his beneficent deeds to the Londoners that he was second only to Becket in the popular estimate, all over southern England. There were pilgrimages from the country around to his shrine in the cathedral, special services on his day, and special hymns. In fact, as in the case of St. Edward, there were two days dedicated to him, that of his death, April 30, and that of his translation, November 14, and these days were classed in London among the high festivals. His costly shrine was at the back of the screen behind the high altar. The inscription upon it, besides enumerating the good deeds we have named, said that he added largely to the noble buildings of the cathedral, greatly enriched its revenues, and obtained for it many privileges from kings. His name, so far as its etymology is concerned, found its repetition in *Archibald*, Bishop of London, 1856—1868, the founder of the " Bishop of London's Fund."

Another bishop of these early times was Theodred, who was named " the Good." We cannot give the exact dates of his episcopate, further than that he was in the See in the middle of the tenth century, as is shown by some charters that he witnessed. There is a pathetic story told of him that on his way from London to join King Athelstan in the north he came to St. Edmund's Bury, and found some men who were charged with robbing the shrine of St. Edmund, and were detected by the Saint's miraculous interference. The bishop ordered them to be hanged; but the uncanonical act weighed so heavily on his conscience that he performed a lifelong penance, and as an expiation reared a splendid shrine over the saint's body. And further, he persuaded the King to decree, in a Witanagemote, that no one younger than fifteen should be put to death for theft. The bishop was buried in the crypt of St. Paul's, and the story was often told at his tomb, which was much frequented by the citizens, of his error and his life-long sorrow.

Another bishop who had been placed in the See by Edward the Confessor, who, it will be remembered, greatly favoured Normans, to the indignation of the English people, was known as "William the Norman," and, unpopular as the appointment may have been, it did the English good service. For when the Norman Conquest came the Londoners, for a while, were in fierce antagonism, and it might have gone hard with them. But Bishop William was known to the Conqueror, and had, in fact, been his chaplain, and it was by his intercession that he not only made friends with them, but gave them the charter still to be seen at the Guildhall. His monument was in the nave, towards the west end, and told that he was " vir sapientia et vitæ sanctitate clarus." He was bishop for twenty years, and died in 1075. The following tribute on the stone is worth preserving :—

"Hæc tibi, clare Pater, posuerunt marmora cives,
    Præmia non meritis æquiparanda tuis :
Namque sibi populus te Londoniensis amicum
    Sensit, et huic urbi non leve presidium :
Reddita Libertas, duce te, donataque multis,
    Te duce, res fuerat publica muneribus.
Divitias, genus, et formam brevis opprimat hora,
    Hæc tua sed pietas et benefacta manent." *

To his shrine also an annual pilgrimage was made, and Lord Mayor Barkham, on renewing the above inscription A.D. 1622, puts in a word for himself :

"This being by Barkham's thankful mind renewed,
Call it the monument of gratitude."

* " This humble tomb our citizens placed here
    Unequal to thy merits, father dear;
For London's people know how wisely thou
    Didst guide their fate, and gladly feel it now.
Under thy guidance freedom was restored,
    And noble gifts through thee on us were poured.
Riches and earthly honours cease to be,
    But thy good deeds abide in memory."

We pass on to the time of the "second church," the Old St. Paul's which is the subject of this monograph.

The importance of London had been growing without interruption ever since its restoration by King Alfred, and it had risen to its position as the capital city. This largely showed itself when Archbishop Lanfranc, in 1075, held a great council in St. Paul's, "the first full Ecclesiastical Parliament of England," Dean Milman calls it. Up to that time, secular and Church matters had been settled in the same assembly, but this meeting, held with the King's sanction, and simultaneously with the Witan, or Parliament, established distinct courts for the trial of ecclesiastical causes. It decreed that no bishop or archdeacon should sit in the shiremote or hundred-mote, and that no layman should try causes pertaining to the cure of souls. The same council removed some episcopal sees from villages to towns, Selsey to Chichester, Elmham first to Thetford, then to Norwich, Sherburn to Old Sarum, Dorchester-on-Thame to Lincoln.

Another council of the great men met in St. Paul's in the course of the dispute between Henry I. and Anselm about the investitures, but it ended in a deadlock, and a fresh appeal to the Pope.

In the fierce struggle between Henry II. and Archbishop Becket, Gilbert Foliot, Bishop of London, while apparently quite honest in his desire to uphold the rights of the Church, also remained in favour with the King, and hoped to bring about peace. Becket regarded Foliot as his bitter enemy, and, whilst the latter was engaged in the most solemn service in St. Paul's (on St. Paul's Day, 1167), an emissary from the Archbishop, who was then in self-imposed exile abroad, came up to the altar, thrust a sentence of excommunication into his hands, and exclaimed aloud, "Know all men that Gilbert, Bishop of London, is excommunicated by Thomas, Archbishop of Canterbury." When Becket returned to England, December 1st, 1170, after a hollow reconciliation with the King, he was asked to remove his sentence of excommunication on Foliot and the Bishops of Salisbury and York, who had, as he held, usurped his authority. He refused, unless they made acknowledgment of their errors. The sequel we know. The King's hasty exclamation on hearing of this brought about the Archbishop's murder on the 29th of the same month.

During the excommunication, Foliot seems to have behaved wisely and well. He refused to accept it as valid, but stayed away from the cathedral to avoid giving offence to sensitive consciences. After Becket's murder, he declared his innocence of any share in it, and the Bishop of Nevers removed the sentence of excommunication.

It was at this period that the Deanery was occupied by the first man of letters it had yet possessed, Ralph de Diceto. His name is a puzzle ; no one has as yet ascertained the place from which it is taken. Very probably he was of foreign birth. When Belmeis was made Bishop of London in 1152, Diceto succeeded him as Archdeacon of Middlesex. His learning was great, and his chronicles (which have been edited by Bishop Stubbs) are of great historical value. In the Becket quarrel Diceto was loyal to Foliot, but he also remained friendly with Becket. In 1180, he became Dean of St. Paul's. Here he displayed great and most valuable energy; made a survey of the capitular property (printed by the Camden Society under the editorship of Archdeacon Hale), collected many books, which he presented to the Chapter, built a Deanery House, and established a "fratery," or guild for the ministration to the spiritual and bodily wants of the sick and poor. He died in 1202. He wrote against the strict views concerning the celibacy of the clergy promulgated by Pope Gregory VII., and declared that the doctrine and the actual practice made a great scandal to the laity. Dean Milman suspects that he was much moved herein by the condition of his own Chapter.

In 1191, whilst King Richard I. was in Palestine, his brother John summoned a council to St. Paul's to denounce William de Longchamp, Bishop of Ely, to whom Richard had entrusted the affairs of government, of high crimes and misdemeanours. The result was that Longchamp had to escape across sea. At length the King returned, but the Londoners were deeply disaffected. William FitzOsbert, popularly known as "Longbeard," poured forth impassioned harangues from Paul's Cross against the oppression of the poor, and the cathedral was invaded by rioters. Fifty-two thousand persons bound themselves to follow him, but Hubert, Archbishop of Canterbury, met the citizens in the cathedral, and by his mild and persuasive eloquence persuaded them to preserve the peace. FitzOsbert, finding himself deserted, clove

the head of the man sent to arrest him, and shut himself up in the
church of St. Mary-le-Bow. His followers kept aloof, and a three-days'
siege was ended by the church being set on fire. On his attempt to
escape he was severely wounded by the son of the man he had killed,
was dragged away, and burned alive. But his memory was long
cherished by the poor. Paul's Cross was silent for many years from
that time.

In 1213, a great meeting of bishops, abbots, and barons met at
St. Paul's to consider the misgovernment and illegal acts of King
John. Archbishop Langton laid before the assembly the charter of
Henry I., and commented on its provisions. The result was an oath,
taken with acclamation, that they would, if necessary, die for their
liberties. And this led up to Magna Charta. But it was a scene
as ignominious as the first surrender before Pandulf, when Pope
Innocent accepted the homage of King John as the price of supporting
him against his barons, and the wretched King, before the altar of
St. Paul, ceded his kingdom as a fief of the Holy See. The Archbishop of Canterbury protested both privately and publicly against it.

Henry III. succeeded, at the age of ten years, to a crown which his
father had degraded. The Pope addressed him as "Vassallus Noster,"
and sent his legates, one after another, to maintain his authority. It
was in St. Paul's Cathedral that this authority was most conspicuously
asserted. Before the high altar these legates took their seat, issued
canons of doctrine and discipline, and assessed the tribute which clergy
and laity were to pay to the liege lord enthroned at the Vatican. But
the indignation of the nation had been waxing hotter and hotter ever
since King John's shameful surrender. Nevertheless, in the first days
of the boy King's reign, the Papal pretensions did good service. The
barons, in wrath at John's falseness, had invited the intervention of
France, and the Dauphin was now in power. In St. Paul's Cathedral,
half England swore allegiance to him. The Papal legate, Gualo,
by his indignant remonstrance, awoke in them the sense of shame, and
the evil was averted. Then another council was held in the same
cathedral, and the King ratified the Great Charter.

Henry III. grew to manhood, and gave himself up to the management
of foreign favourites, and in 1237, instigated by these, who were led by

Peter de la Roche, Bishop of Winchester, he invited Pope Gregory IX. to
send a Legate (Cardinal Otho "the White") to arrange certain matters
concerning English benefices, as well as some fresh tribute. They called
it "promoting reforms." Their object was to support him in filling all
the rich preferments with the Poitevins and Gascons whom he was
bringing over in swarms. The Cardinal took his lofty seat before the
altar of S. Paul's, and the King bowed before him "until his head almost
touched his knees." The Cardinal "lifted up his voice like a trumpet"
and preached the first sermon of which we have any report in St. Paul's.
His text was Rev. iv. 6, and he interpreted "the living creatures"
as the bishops who surrounded his legatine throne, whose eyes were to
be everywhere and on all sides. The chroniclers tell how a terrific storm
burst over the cathedral at this moment, to the terror of the whole
congregation, including the Legate, and lasted for fifteen days. It did
much harm to the building. The bishop, Roger Niger, exerted himself
strenuously in repairing this. Edmund Rich, the Archbishop of Canterbury, indignantly protested against the intrusion of foreign authority, and
was joined by Walter de Cantelupe, the saintly Bishop of Worcester, but
for a long time they were powerless. Besides direct taxation, wealth raised
from the appropriation of rich canonries was drained away from church
and state into the Papal treasury. The Legate remained for four years
in power. The Archbishop, in despair, retired abroad, and died as a
simple monk at Pontigny. The Bishop of London, Roger Niger,
was so called from his dark complexion, and people whimsically
noted his being confronted with the Cardinal Otto Albus. Bishop
Roger, before his episcopate, was Archdeacon of Rochester, a very
wise and energetic administrator. He was now on the side of Rich,
bent on defending his clergy from being over-ridden by the foreigners.
He exerted himself as bishop not only to repair the mischief done by the
storm, but to enlarge and beautify the still unfinished structure. Fourteen years later King Henry was offering devotion at the shrine of Rich,
for he had been canonised, and that on the strength of his having resisted
the King's criminal folly in betraying the rights of his people ; for by this
time the nation was aroused. The Londoners rose and burned the
houses of the foreigners. Bishop Roger, though he, of course, declared
against the scenes of violence, let it be seen that he was determined,

by constitutional methods, to defend his clergy from being plundered. On his death, in 1241, there was a long vacancy, the King wanting one man and the canons determined on another, and they carried their man, Fulk Bassett, though he was not consecrated for three years. Pope Innocent IV., in 1246, sent a demand of one-third of their income from the resident clergy, and half from non-resident. Bishop Fulk indignantly called a council at St. Paul's, which declared a refusal, and even the King supported him. The remonstrance ended significantly with a call for a General Council. But he was presently engaged in a more serious quarrel. The King forced the monks of Canterbury, on the death of Edmund Rich, to elect the queen's uncle, Boniface of Savoy, to the primacy. He came and at once began to enrich himself, went " on visitation" through the country demanding money. The Dean of St. Paul's, Henry of Cornhill, shut the door in his face, Bishop Fulk approving. The old Prior of the Monastery of St. Bartholomew, Smithfield, protested, and the Archbishop, who travelled with a cuirass under his pontifical robe, knocked him down with his fist.* Two canons, whom he forced into St. Paul's chapter, were killed by the indignant populace. The same year (1259) brave Bishop Fulk died of the plague. For years the unholy exactions went on, and again and again one has records of meetings in St. Paul's to resist them.

When Simon de Montfort rose up against the evil rule of Henry III. the Londoners met in folkmote, summoned by the great bell of St. Paul's, and declared themselves on the side of the great patriot. They are said to have tried to sink the queen's barge when she was escaping from London to join the King at Windsor.

King Edward I. demanded a moiety of the clerical incomes for his war with Scotland. The Dean of St. Paul's (Montfort) rose to protest against the exaction, and fell dead as he was speaking. Two years later, the King more imperiously demanded it, and Archbishop Winchelsey wrote to the Bishop of London (Gravesend) commanding him to summon the whole of the London clergy to St. Paul's to protest, and to publish the famous Bull, " clericis laicos," of Pope Boniface VIII., which forbade any emperor, king, or prince to tax the clergy without express leave of the Pope. Any layman who exacted, or any cleric who paid, was at

* See *Mediæval London*, p. 62.

once excommunicate. Boniface, who had been pope two years, put forward far more arrogant pretensions than Gregory or Innocent had done, but times were changed. The Kings of England and France were at once in opposition. The latter (Philip IV.) was more cautious than his English neighbour, and in the uncompromising struggle between king and pope, the latter died of grief at defeat, and his successor was compelled, besides making other concessions, to remove the papal residence from Rome to Avignon, where it continued for seventy years, the popes being French nominees. King Edward, with some trouble, got his money, but promised to repay it when the war was over, and the clergy succeeded in wresting some additional privileges from him, which they afterwards used to advantage.

We pass over the unhappy reign of Edward II., only noting that the Bishop of Exeter, Stapylton, who was ruling for him in London, was dragged out of St. Paul's, where he had taken sanctuary, and beheaded in Cheapside. He was the founder of Exeter College, Oxford.

The exile of the popes to Avignon, so far from diminishing their rapacity, increased it, if possible, and Green shows that the immense outlay on their grand palace there caused the passing of the Statute of Provisors in 1350, for the purpose of stopping the incessant draining away of English wealth to the papacy. During that "seventy years' captivity," as it was called, Italy and Rome were revolutionised, and when at length the popes returned to their ancient city (1376) the great "papal schism" began, which did so much to bring on the Reformation. It arose out of the Roman people's determination to have an Italian pope, and the struggle of the French cardinals to keep the dignity for Frenchmen. The momentous results of that fierce conflict only concern us here indirectly. We simply note now that the year following the return to Rome saw John Wyclif brought to account at St. Paul's.

But before following that history, it will not be out of place to take another survey of our cathedral during these years, apart from fightings and controversies. St. Paul's had been most closely connected with the continually growing prosperity of the city. The Lord Mayor was constantly worshipping there in state with his officers. On the 29th of October each year (the morrow of SS. Simon and Jude) he took his oath of office at the Court of Exchequer, dined in public, and, with the aldermen, proceeded from the church of St. Thomas Acons (where the Mercers' Chapel now is) to the cathedral. There a requiem was said for Bishop William, as already described,* then they went on to the tomb of Thomas Becket's parents, and the requiem was again said. This done they returned by Cheapside to the Church of St. Thomas Acons, where each man offered a penny. On All Saints' Day (three days later) they went to St. Paul's again for Vespers, and again at Christmas, on the Epiphany, and on Candlemas Day (Purification). On Whitsun Monday they met at St. Peter's, Cornhill, and on this occasion the City clergy all joined the procession, and again they assembled in the cathedral nave, while the *Veni Creator Spiritus* was sung antiphonally, and a chorister, robed as an angel, waved incense from the rood screen above.† Next day the same ceremony was repeated, but this time it was "the common folk" who joined in the procession, which returned by Newgate, and finished at the Church of St. Michael le Querne.‡ And once more they went through the ceremony, the "common folk of Essex" this time assisting. There could not be fuller proof of the sense of religious duty in civil and commercial life. The history of the City Guilds is full of the same interweaving of the life of the people with the duties of religion. There is an amusing incident recorded of one of these Pentecostal functions. On Whitsun Monday, 1382, John Sely, Alderman of Walbrook, wore a cloak without a lining. It ought to have been lined with green taffeta. There was a meeting of the Council about this, and they gave sentence that the mayor and aldermen should dine with the offender at his cost on the following Thursday, and that he should line his cloak. "And so it was done."

At one of these Whitsun festivals (it was in 1327) another procession was held, no doubt to the delight of many spectators. A roguish baker had a hole made in his table with a door to it, which could be opened and shut at pleasure. When his customers brought dough to be baked he had a confederate under the table who craftily withdrew great pieces. He and some other roguish bakers were tried at the

* Page 25.

† There was a special order in the first year of Edward VI. that instead of this censing a sermon should be preached.

‡ It stood where the Peel statue now is, at the top of Cheapside

MONUMENT OF BISHOP ROGER NIGER. *After W. Hollar.*

MONUMENT OF SIR JOHN BEAUCHAMP, POPULARLY KNOWN AS DUKE HUMPHREY'S. *After W. Hollar.*

BRASS OF RALPH DE HENGHAM.

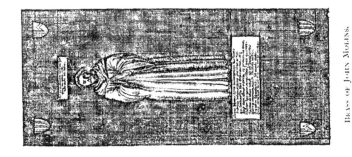

BRASS OF JOHN MOLINS.

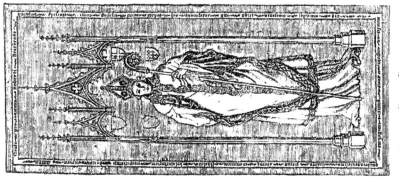

BRASS OF BISHOP BRAYBROOKE.

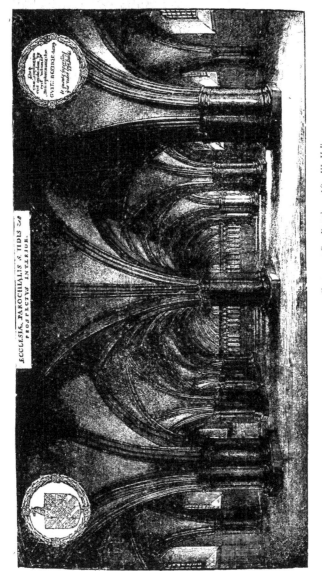

CHURCH OF ST. FAITH IN THE CRYPT OF ST. PAUL'S. *After W. Hollar.*

Guildhall, and ordered to be set in the pillory, in Cheapside, with lumps
of dough round their necks, and there to remain till vespers at St. Paul's
were ended.

We return to the religious history, in which we left off with the name
of Wyclif. The Norman despotism of the Crown was crumbling away,
so was the Latin despotism of the Church. On both sides there was
evident change at hand, and Wiclif gave form to the new movement.
He was born about 1324, educated at Oxford, where he won high
distinction, not only by his learning, but by his holiness of life. The
unparalleled ravages of the plague known as the "black death," not
only in England but on the Continent, affected him so deeply that he
was possessed by the absolute conviction that the wrath of God was
upon the land for the sins of the nation at large, and especially of
the Church, and he began his work as a preacher against the abuses.
His first assault was upon the Mendicant Friars, whom he held up,
as did his contemporary, Chaucer, to the scorn of the world. Then
he passed on to the luxury in which some of the prelates were living,
and to their overweening influence in the Councils of State. Edward III.,
after a reign of great splendour, had sunk into dotage. John of Gaunt
had been striving for mastery against the Black Prince, but the latter
was dying, July, 1376, and Gaunt was now supreme. He hated good
William of Wykeham, who had possessed enormous influence with the
old king, and he was bent generally on curbing the power of the higher
clergy. At this juncture Wyclif was summoned to appear at St. Paul's
to answer for certain opinions which he had uttered. It is not clear what
these opinions were, further than that they were mainly against clerical
powers and assumptions ; questions of doctrine had not yet shaped
themselves. He appeared before the tribunal, but not alone. Gaunt
stood by his side. And here, for a while, the position of parties becomes
somewhat complicated. Gaunt was at this moment very unpopular.
The Black Prince was the favourite hero of the multitude, an unworthy
one indeed, as Dean Kitchin has abundantly shown, but he had won
great victories, and had been handsome and gracious in manners. He
was now at the point of death, and Gaunt was believed to be aiming at
the succession, to the exclusion of the Black Prince's son, and was asso-
ciated in the popular mind with the King's mistress, Alice Ferrers, as

taking every sort of mean and wicked advantage of the old man's dotage.
Added to this the Londoners were on the side of their Bishop (Courtenay)
in defence, as they held, of the rights of the City.   So on the day
of Wyclif's appearance the cathedral and streets surrounding it were
crowded, to such an extent indeed that Wyclif had much trouble in
getting through, and when Gaunt was seen, accompanied by his large
body of retainers, a wild tumult ensued ; the mob attacked Gaunt's
noble mansion, the Savoy Palace, and had not Courtenay intervened,
would have burnt it down.   The Black Prince's widow was at her
palace at Kennington, with her son, the future Richard II., and her great
influence was able to pacify the rioters.

Soon came an overwhelming change.   The succession of the Black
Prince's son was secured, and then public opinion was directed to the
other question, Wyclif's denunciation of the Papal abuses.   Relieved from
Gaunt's partisanship, he sprang at once into unbounded popularity.   His
learning, his piety of life, were fully recognised, and the Londoners were
now on his side.   He had preached at the very beginning of the new
reign that a great amount of treasure, in the hands of the Pope's agent,
ought not to pass out of England.   Archbishop Sudbury summoned him
not to St. Paul's, but to Lambeth.   But the favour with which he was
now regarded was so manifest that he was allowed to depart from the
assembly a free man, only with an injunction to keep silence " lest
he should mislead the ignorant."   He went back to Lutterworth, where
he occupied himself in preaching and translating the Bible.   He died in
1384.   A wonderful impetus was, however, given to the spread of his
opinions by the schism in the Papacy which was filling Europe with
horrified amazement.

From that time till the accession of the Tudors, two subjects are
prominent in English history : the spread of Lollardism, *i.e.*, the
Wycliffite doctrines, and the Wars of the Roses.   Both topics have some
place in the history of Old St. Paul's.

Richard II. on his accession came in great pomp hither, and never
again alive.   But his body was shown in the cathedral by his victorious
successor, Henry IV., who had a few days before buried his father, John
of Gaunt, there, who died at Ely House, Holborn, February 3rd, 1399,
and whose tomb was one of the finest in the cathedral, as sumptuous

as those of his father, Edward III., at Westminster, and his son, Henry IV., at Canterbury.

Humphrey, Duke of Gloucester, the youngest son of Henry IV., was appointed guardian of his infant nephew, Henry VI., on his father's death ; but partly though the intrigues and squabbles of the royal family, partly by his own mismanagement, he lost the confidence of the nation. His wife, Jacqueline, had been persuaded by a sorcerer that her husband would be king, and she joined him in acts of witchcraft in order to bring this about. She was condemned (October, 1441) to do penance by walking three successive days in a white sheet and carrying a lighted taper, starting each day from St. Paul's and visiting certain churches. Her husband, says the chronicler Grafton, "took all patiently and said little." Still retaining some power in .the Council, he lived until 1447, when he died and was buried at St. Albans. He was an unprincipled man, but a generous patron of letters and a persecutor of Lollards ; and hence, in after years, he got the name of " the good Duke Humphrey," which was hardly a greater delusion than that which afterwards identified the tomb of Sir John Beauchamp in St. Paul's as Duke Humphrey's. But the strange error was accepted, and the aisle in which the said tomb lay was commonly known as " Duke Humphrey's Walk," and it was a favourite resort of insolvent debtors and beggars, who loitered about it dinnerless and in hope of alms. And thus arose the phrase of " Dining with Duke Humphrey," *i.e.*, going without ; a phrase, it will be seen, founded on a strange blunder. The real grave is on the south side of the shrine of St. Alban's.

Richard, Duke of York, swore fealty in most express terms to Henry VI. at St. Paul's in March, 1452. He had been suspected of aiming at the crown. But the government grew so unpopular, partly through the disasters in France, partly through the King's incapacity, that York levied an army and demanded " reformation of the Government." And on May 23rd, 1455, was fought the battle of St. Albans, the first of twelve pitched battles, the first blood spilt in a fierce contest which lasted for thirty years, and almost destroyed the ancient nobility of England. York himself was killed at Wakefield, December 23rd, 1460. On the following 3rd of March his son was proclaimed King Edward IV. in London, and on the 29th (Palm Sunday) he defeated Henry's Queen

Margaret at Towton, the bloodiest battle ever fought on English ground. A complicated struggle followed, during which there was much changing of sides. Once King Henry, who had been imprisoned in the Tower, was brought out by the Earl of Warwick, who had changed sides, and conducted to St. Paul's in state. But the Londoners showed that they had no sympathy; they were on the Yorkist side in the interest of strong government. Hall the chronicler makes an amusing remark on Warwick's parading of King Henry in the streets. "It no more moved the Londoners," he says, "than the fire painted on the wall warmed the old woman." That is worthy of Sam Weller. In May, 1470, Henry died in the Tower, and his corpse was exhibited in St. Paul's. It was alleged that as it lay there blood flowed from the nose as Richard Crookback entered, witnessing that he was the murderer. Richard afterwards came again to offer his devotions after the death of his brother, Edward IV., and all the while he was planning the murder of his young nephews.

Arthur, Prince of Wales, son of Henry VII., married Catharine of Aragon in St. Paul's, November 14th, 1501. He died five months later, at the age of 15. The chroniclers are profuse in their descriptions of the decorations of the cathedral and city on that occasion. The body of Henry VII. lay in state at St. Paul's before it was buried in Westminster Abbey.

This brings us to a new epoch altogether in our history. The stirring events now to be noted do not so much concern the material fabric of the cathedral as in the past, but they were of the most momentous interest, and St. Paul's took more part in them than did any other cathedral.

CHAPTER V. ·

Good Dean Colet — Accession of Henry VIII. — Papal Favour — Cardinal Wolsey at St. Paul's — Bishop Fisher's Preaching at Paul's Cross — Fall of Wolsey — Alienation of the King from the Pope — The English Bible in the Cathedral — — Edward VI. — Ridley's Strong Protest against the Images — Progress of the Reformed Doctrines — Somerset's Evil Deeds — Destruction of the Cloisters — Re-establishment of the Roman Mass under Mary — Cardinal Pole at St. Paul's — The Lord Mayor's Proclamation — Alienation of the Nation from Romanism — Death of Mary and Accession of Elizabeth — The Reformed Liturgy Restored — Growth of Puritanism — Destruction of the Steeple by Lightning — Continued Irreverence — Retrospect, the Tudor Monuments.

IT seems fitting that we should open the chapter of a new era in the history of St. Paul's with the name of its most famous Dean, a great, wise, good man. His name was John Colet. He was born in London, in the year 1466, within three months of his famous friend, Erasmus. His father, Sir Henry Colet, was twice Lord Mayor, one of the richest members of the Mercers' Company. John, who was his eldest son, had ten brothers and eleven sisters, all by the same mother, who outlived the last of them. The young man was presented to livings (it was no unusual thing then) before he took Orders, and gave himself to study, both mathematical and classical, and in his zeal for learning travelled much abroad, where he saw much of ecclesiastical life, which startled him greatly. Returning, at length, to England, he was ordained at Christmas, 1497, went to Oxford, and began to lecture with great power on the Epistle to the Romans. It must be remembered that this was the epoch when the fall of Constantinople had driven the Greek scholars westward, the epoch of the revival of "the new learning" in Europe, the discrediting of the old scholastic philosophy which was now worn out and ready to vanish away. Colet stands before us then as the representative of the new learning in England, and as keen to reform the abuses in the Church which were terrifying all earnest and thoughtful men. He carried on his lectures with such energy that his lecture-room was crowded, the most distinguished tutors there being among his audience. And one day there came the great Erasmus, who had heard of him, and from the day of their first meeting they were fast friends for life. In 1504, Henry VII. made Colet Dean of St. Paul's, and he showed at once that he had lost none of his zeal. He carried on his lectures in the cathedral and preached constantly, and another warm friend made now was Sir Thomas More, who earnestly helped him in his strenuous endeavours to improve the cathedral statutes, to reform abuses, and to increase the preaching power. He was a rich man, and in 1509 he employed much of his wealth—about £40,000 present value—in the foundation of St. Paul's School. He wrote some simple precepts for the guidance of masters and scholars, and drew up prayers and an English version of the Creed. He appointed William Lilly first master, and called on Linacre to write a Latin grammar. The school became famous; it was burnt down in the Fire, rebuilt in 1670, and removed to Hammersmith in 1884. It is not to be wondered at that many of the churchmen of the day regarded Colet as a most dangerous innovator. Complaints were made to Archbishop Warham that he was favouring the Lollards, which was absolutely untrue. He would in all probability, had he lived, have been found on the same side as More and Fisher, that is, intensely desirous to preserve the Church and its doctrines, but to cleanse it from the foul scandals, the sloth, greed, immorality, which were patent to all the world. There was a meeting of Convocation in February, 1512, to consider how to extirpate the Lollard heresy which was reviving. Warham appointed Colet to preach the sermon, which he did with wonderful energy, denouncing the simony, the self-indulgence, and the ignorance of the bishops and clergy. The Lollards were there in great numbers, attentive, silent listeners. He was as plain and honest with the King himself, who, recognising his goodness of purpose, made him a Royal Chaplain. In 1514, he went with Erasmus on pilgrimage to Becket's tomb and ridiculed the accounts which the vergers gave of the healing power of the relics. When

Wolsey was installed as Cardinal, Colet preached, and warned him against worldly ambition. And all through his time at St. Paul's the aged Bishop Fitzhugh was in active hostility to him. He died September 16th, 1519, and, although he had requested that only his name should be inscribed on his grave, the Mercers' Company erected a handsome tomb, for which Lilly wrote a long inscription. Lilly and Linacre were both buried near him.

It will be seen, I think, at once that Colet is a great representative of the thoughtful and earnest men of his time, one of the greatest precursors of the Reformers, or rather, in full sense, a great reformer himself. We have now to take up the course of secular events. In 1514, Pope Leo X. sent young King Henry VIII. a " sword and cap of maintenance " as a special honour, and he, " in robe of purple, satin, and gold in chequer, and jewelled collar," came to the Bishop's palace, and from thence there was a grand procession of gorgeously-arrayed nobles and clerics round the church, with joyous hymns.

Four years later came Wolsey, and sang High Mass to celebrate eternal peace between England, France, and Spain. The King's beautiful sister, Mary, was betrothed at the same time to Louis XII., who was fifty-three years old, while she was sixteen. Within three months he died, and she married Charles Brandon, Duke of Suffolk, and became grandmother of Lady Jane Grey. Again one comes on a full description of the gorgeous ceremonial. A year later, the accession of Charles V. was announced by the Heralds in St. Paul's, and Wolsey pronounced a benediction. The great Cardinal was now in full hopes of the papal tiara ; the same year he came in state (May 12th, 1521) with the Archbishop of Canterbury, Warham, to hear Bishop Fisher denounce Luther at Paul's Cross, with accompanying appropriate ceremonies. An account on a broad-sheet in the British Museum tells how Wolsey came with the most part of the bishops of the realm, "where he was received with procession and censed by Mr. Richard Pace, Dean of the said church." Pace was a native of Winchester, who had won the favour of two successive bishops of that See, and been educated by them. One of them sent him to the Continent to complete his course. He took

Orders in 1510, and his evident ability induced Wolsey to employ
him in more than one delicate and difficult case of foreign
diplomacy, and also brought him to the favourable notice of the
King, who, after many other preferments, made him Dean of
St. Paul's on the death of Colet.   He was held to be the very
ablest of diplomatists, was a friend of Erasmus, and followed Colet
in favouring "the new learning."   It was he and Sir T. More who
persuaded the King to found Greek professorships at Oxford and
Cambridge.

   But to return to the ceremony at St. Paul's.   "After the Dean had
duly censed him, the Cardinal, while four doctors bore a canopy of gold
over him, went to the high altar, where he made his obligation ;
which done, he went, as before, to the Cross in the churchyard,
where was a scaffold set up.   On this he seated himself under his
cloth of estate, his two crosses on each side of him ; on his right
hand, sitting on the place where he set his feet, the Pope's
ambassador, and next him the Archbishop of Canterbury ; on his
left hand, the Emperor's ambassador, and next him the Bishop of
Durham (Rusthall) ; and all the other bishops, with other noble
prelates, sat on two forms out right forth, and then the Bishop of
Rochester made a sermon by the consenting of the whole clergy of
England, by the commandment of the Pope, against one *Martinus
Eleutherus* and all his works, because he erred sore, and spake against
the Holy Faith ; and denounced them accursed which kept any of
his books ; and there were many burned in the said churchyard of
his said books during the sermon.   Which ended, my Lord Cardinal
went home to dinner with all the other prelates."

   The Bishop of Rochester was, of course, Fisher.   He was both
learned and pious.   Burnet says he strongly disliked Wolsey, because
of the latter's notoriously immoral life.   Fisher, though in his
unflinching conservatism he regarded the proceedings of Luther with
hostility, was anxious, as were More and Erasmus and Colet, for
reformation on Catholic lines.   He, like them, favoured the new
learning, and even declared that the Continental reformers had brought
much light to bear upon religion.   But he opposed the King's
divorce, and refused to acknowledge his supremacy over the Church,

and was beheaded on Tower Hill, June 22nd, 1535. There was no act of Henry which more thoroughly excited popular horror.

When Charles V. came to England, in 1522, Wolsey again said Mass at St. Paul's, with twenty bishops to cense him. It was on this occasion that he changed the meeting-place of Convocation from St. Paul's to Westminster, that it might be near his own house. Skelton, the poet, who hated Wolsey, thereupon wrote the following distich :—

> "Gentle Paul, lay down thy sword,
>   For Peter, of Westminster, hath shaven thy beard."

In 1524, Francis I. was taken prisoner at the battle of Pavia, whereupon the sympathy of England for his successful rival was shown by a huge bonfire in front of St. Paul's, and the distribution of many hogsheads of claret. On the Sunday following, Wolsey sang Mass, and the King and Queen, with both Houses of Parliament, were present. Once more (Shrove Tuesday, 1527) the great Cardinal came in dignity; it was to denounce the translation of the Bible and to condemn the Lutherans. Certain " heretics " were marched through the cathedral in penitential dresses, and carrying faggots, which they threw into the fire by the great rood at the north door, in which Testaments and Lutheran tracts were also burned. On this occasion, also, Fisher preached the sermon. A few years later (1530), there was a similar holocaust, at which the Bishop (Stokesley) presided.

But now came an event of momentous importance. Wolsey fell into disgrace with the King, and, after some preliminary attacks, was charged with high treason. From trial on this charge he was delivered by death (November 28th, 1530). But he had brought the clergy unwittingly into trouble. The law of *Præmunire* forbade a man to accept the office of papal legate in England, or the clergy to recognise him. Wolsey had obtained a patent under the Great Seal to exercise legatine authority, and for fifteen years no objection had been taken. When he was indicted for the infringement of the law, he refused to plead royal permission, fearing to incur yet greater displeasure of the King. So judgment went by default. And now the clergy were likewise impeached. They met in St. Paul's Chapter House, and in their terror offered £100,000 fine, under the advice of the Bishop. The King refused to accept this unless they recognised him as "supreme head of the Church." Three days' discussion of this proposition followed, then, on the proposal of Archbishop Warham, they agreed to the following :—"of which Church and clergy we acknowledge his Majesty to be the chief protector, the only supreme lord, and, as far as the law of Christ will allow, the supreme head." Such a compromise meant nothing, for it did not attempt to define what the law of Christ on the subject was. But it was evident that the Reformation had begun in earnest. Though nineteen Anabaptists were condemned in St. Paul's to be burned, and on fourteen of them the sentence was carried out, Paul's Cross echoed with renunciation of the Pope's authority. The miraculous rood of Bexley, in Kent, having been exposed as a fraud there, was brought up to Paul's Cross, February, 1538, and the mechanism having been shown to the indignant audience, it was committed to the flames.

A more significant indication of the coming change was witnessed in 1541. In May of the previous year, King Henry issued a proclamation that every parish in England should provide itself with a copy of the English Bible by All-hallow-tide next, under a penalty of 40s. He explains that the object is that "the power, wisdom, and goodness of God may be perceived hereby," but the people are not to expound it, nor to read it while Mass is going on, but are to "read it meekly, humbly, and reverently for their instruction, edification, and amendment." Accordingly, Bishop Bonner had six of these great Bibles chained to pillars in different parts of St. Paul's, as well as an "advertisement" fixed at the same places, "admonishing all that came thither to read that they should lay aside vain-glory, hypocrisy, and all other corrupt affections, and bring with them discretion, good intention, charity, reverence, and a quiet behaviour, for the edification of their own souls; but not to draw multitudes about them, nor to make exposition of what they read, nor to read aloud in time of divine service, nor enter into disputes concerning it."

There was no mistake as to the eagerness of the people to take advantage of the opportunity. They assembled in crowds to hear such as could read, and even, so says Burnet, sent their children to school that they might carry them with them and hear them read.

It is not to be wondered at that Bonner soon found that his Advertisement was powerless to check what he dreaded. Not only did expounders dwell upon such words as "Drink ye all of it," but they compared the clergy to the Scribes and Pharisees, and identified them with the generation of vipers, and with priests of Baal. Accordingly, he put forth a fresh advertisement, in which he said that "diverse, wilful, and unlearned persons, contrary to all good order and honest behaviour, have read the Scriptures especially and chiefly at the time of divine service in this right honourable Catholic church, yea, in the time of the sermon and declaration of the Word of God, in such sort as was both to the evil and lewd example of the rest of the multitude, and also to the high dishonour of the Word of God, over and beside the great disturbance and unquietness of the people repairing hither for honest purposes." And he declares that if this friendly admonition be not attended to he will have the Bibles removed, but that he shall do so very unwillingly, seeing that he "will be, by God's grace, right glad that the Scripture and Word of God should be well known."

There is a painful story in "Foxe's Martyrs," that one John Porter was thrown into Newgate by Bonner for thus "expounding," and that he died there of the ill-treatment he received.

In the short reign of Edward VI., great destruction was wrought in the structure and ornamentation of St. Paul's, and no thanks are due to the "Protector" that the mischief was not greater. There was no sign for a month or two. Edward ascended the throne on January 28, 1547, and just two months later the French king, Francis I., died. On that occasion, Cranmer, attended by eight bishops, sang a Requiem Mass in Latin at St. Paul's, and Gardiner preached a funeral sermon before the Lord Mayor and Aldermen, eulogising this persecutor of the Reformed Faith. But now came unmistakable signs of change. Ridley, then Master of Pembroke College, Cambridge, soon to be Bishop of London, preached a somewhat violent sermon at Paul's Cross against the adoration of saints, the use of holy water, and the reverence done to pictures and images. We may note that on the day of the King's Coronation, amid all the splendid pageantry and decorations, a cable was fastened to the top of St. Paul's steeple, the other end attached to an anchor by the Deanery door, and a sailor descended "swift as an arrow from the bow."

It was in September following that the order from the Council commanded the destruction of images in churches and the discontinuance of all processions. The Bishop, Bonner, protested against the alterations and was sent to the Fleet for contumacy, made submission, and was released after eight days, during which the alterations were made. The images were all pulled down, as were the rood, the crucifix, and its attendants, St. Mary and St. John.

The "Grey Friars Chronicle" * (published by the Camden Society), describes all this, and takes care to note that two of the men engaged in the sacrilegious work were killed. The almsboxes shared the general confiscation, and doubtless not only the services of the church, but the poor who came for food, suffered thereby.

Protector Somerset had wide ideas. He aspired to build himself a magnificent palace and to attach a park to it along the banks of the Thames. The palace was on the site of the present Somerset House; the park was to extend from it to St. Paul's. The cloister and chapel in Pardon Churchyard were destroyed, and five hundred tons of bones were carted away to Finsbury Fields (it is said there were more than a thousand cartloads) and piled up into a mound, which got the name of the "Bone Hill," and this has come in our day to "Bunhill." On this hill three windmills were erected. The mound has long since been trodden down, and the windmills are gone, but the name "Windmill Street" remains. The chapter house and the small cloister round it, of which we have already spoken, were also destroyed, and the materials were used for the new Somerset House. Within the last few years the bases of parts of this cloister have been uncovered under the skilful supervision of Mr. Penrose, and may be seen on the south side of the present cathedral.

* The Grey Friars Monastery was on the site of Christ's Hospital, this year removed. The Chronicler was one of the expelled monks, and, naturally enough, was shocked at the whole business.

As our subject is only the cathedral itself, we pass by the controversies and changes in creed and practice which the reign of Edward VI. witnessed. The Protector Somerset fell the victim of his own inordinate covetousness, and died on the scaffold, January 22nd, 1552, to the great satisfaction of the "Grey Friar" chronicler. But the Reformation went on; Bonner was imprisoned all through the reign, Ridley was made Bishop of London (1550), and the sacrament was administered according to the Reformed use. Rood-loft, altars, crucifixes, images, all disappeared. The Dean, William May, gave orders for the removal of the organ, but they were not carried out. It pealed out the *Te Deum* on the accession of Mary, July 6th, 1553. The nation certainly rejoiced at this change. Not merely the rapacity of the ruling powers at court had alienated public sympathy, but the people at large at this time resented the loss of their ancient worship, and had not as yet learned the greater spirituality and reality of the Reformed service. We may note that in the exuberance of popular delight in London whilst the cathedral bells were ringing, a Dutchman went to the very top of the lofty steeple, waved a flag, and kindled a blaze of torches.

But a fierce contest was inevitable. Paul's Cross for a little while gave forth most conflicting views. Before the year was out the mass was re-established in St. Paul's. On St. Catharine's Day there were splendid processions and stately ceremonial, with special thought of the Queen's mother, Catharine of Aragon. In a word, it was in St. Paul's Cathedral that the recovery of Roman Catholicism was specially manifested in England. William May was deprived of the Deanery, he being a hearty supporter of the Reformed doctrines, and Feckenham succeeded him, but in 1556 was made Abbot of Westminster. He was so holy and kindly a man that he won great respect, though he was an uncompromising Papist. He is said to have so exerted himself with Queen Mary to procure the liberation of her sister Elizabeth as to offend the Queen, and it is further said (Fuller) that Elizabeth on her accession sent for him and offered him the Archbishopric of Canterbury if he would conform to the Reformed Faith. He refused, and was deprived, and went into retirement, and at St. Paul's May was restored to the Deanery.

At the time of his deprivation, as I have said, St. Paul's at once furnished proof of the restoration of the Roman faith. The great rood was set up with stately ceremonial, in preparation for the visit of the Queen and her husband, Philip of Spain, they having been married at Winchester, July 29th, 1554. On their state visit to St. Paul's, September 30th following, the greatest congregation that had ever yet assembled there was gathered to see them. But as great, so says Machyn*, assembled again on the first Sunday in Advent to receive Cardinal Pole as Papal Legate. Three days before, on the Feast of St. Andrew, he had absolved England at Westminster Hall, and received it back to Communion. Now, having landed at Baynard's Castle Wharf, he was conducted by the Lord Mayor and Aldermen, Lord Chancellor and Bishops, all in splendid procession, followed by a retinue of nobles and knights, with the legate's cross carried before him, King Philip and Queen Mary walking by his side on the right hand and the left. Gardiner preached at Paul's Cross, the first part penitent, the latter exultant, and ending with the words, " Verily this is the great day of the ,Lord."

Of one passage in the history of this time we can speak with unqualified approval. On August 5th, 1554, the Lord Mayor (White) issued the following Proclamation :—

"Forasmuch as the material temples or churches of God were first ordained and instituted and made in all places for the lawful and devout assembly of the people there to lift up their hearts and to laud and praise Almighty God and to hear His Divine Service and most holy Word and Gospel sincerely said, sung, and taught, and not to be used as market places or other profane places, or common thoroughfares with carriage of things ; and that now of late years many of the inhabitants of this City of London, and other people repairing to the same, have and yet do commonly use and accustom themselves very unseemly and unreverently ; the more is the pity to make the common carriage of great vessels full of ale and beer, great baskets full of bread, fish, fruit, and such other things,

* Robert Machyn was an upholsterer of Queenhithe, whose business, however, was chiefly in the way of funerals. He kept a diary, which is much used by Strype in his *Annals*, but has been reprinted in full by the Camden Society. It is very amusing, very illiterate, and full of gossip. He was a hot partisan of the Roman faith, and so never loses the opportunity of a fling at the Reformers. He died of the plague in 1563.

fardels [bundles] of stuff and other gross wares through the Cathedral Church of St. Paul within the said City of London, and some in leading of horses, mules, or other beasts through the same unreverently, to the great dishonour and displeasure of Almighty God, and the great grief also and offence of all good and well-disposed persons. Be it therefore for remedy and reformation thereof ordained, enacted, and established by the Lord Mayor, Aldermen, and Commons in this present Common Council assembled and by the authority of the same, according to the privileges and customs of this ancient city that no manner of person or persons, either free of the said city or foreign, of what estate, condition, or degree soever he or they be, do at any time from henceforth carry, or convey, or cause to be conveyed or carried through the said Cathedral Church of St. Paul any manner of great vessel or vessels, basket or baskets, with bread, ale, beer, flesh, fruit, fish, fardells of stuff, wood billets, faggots, mule, horse, or other beasts, or any other like thing or things, upon pain of forfeiture and losing for every such his or their offence iii*s.* iiij*d.*, and for the second like offence vi*s.* viij*d.*, and for the third offence x*s.*, and for every other offence after such third time to forfeit and lose like sum, and to suffer imprisonment by the space of two whole days and nights without bail or mainprise. The one moiety of all which pains and penalties shall be to the use of the poor called Christ's Hospital within Newgate for the time being, and the other moiety thereof shall be to the use of him or them that will sue for the same in any Court of Record within same City by bill, original plaint, or information, to be commenced and sued in the name of the chamberlains of the said city for the time being, wherein none essoyne [exemption] or wages of law for the defendants shall be admitted or allowed.

"God save the King and Queen."

(Guildhall Records.)

We have had the grand ceremonial at the Reconciliation to Rome. Another procession—oh! the pity of it—was held on St. Paul's Day, 1550, of 160 priests, with Bishop Bonner at the head, singing their thanksgiving that the Queen was about to become a mother, and on the following April 30th, came the report that a prince was born. Again the bells rang out, and solemn *Te Deum* was sung! Machyn

tells of the disappointment which followed, and expresses his hope for
the future, hope not to be fulfilled.

What was it turned the tide of religious opinion? The answer
admits of no doubt. John Rogers, the proto-martyr of the English
Reformation, was a prebendary of St. Paul's, a man of saintly life.
He had given much help to Tyndale, the translator of the Bible, had
brought the MS. to England, and published it. He was sentenced
to be burned only three days after the reception of Pole, and died
with dauntless courage, even his wife and children encouraging him.
In the following October, his Bishop and patron, Ridley, also died the
same fiery death. Machyn records, with apparent callousness, the
burnings which went on in Smithfield day after day, along with trifling
incidents and stately ceremonials at St. Paul's. He does not realise
that these things were horrifying the English people, and turning
their hearts steadfastly to the persecuted faith. The greater number
of the martyr fires took place in London, and St. Paul's was the
place of trial. On the 13th of November, 1558, the Queen issued
a brief to Bonner, giving him command to burn heretics without
mercy, and four days later she died, as, on the same day, did
Cardinal Pole.

The heart of England was alienated from a religion which had
resorted to such brutalities, and the doctrines of the Reformation were
everywhere received. Queen Elizabeth, however, would not be incautious.
There was no immediate interference with the Marian ceremonial. There
was a solemn Requiem Mass sung at St. Paul's after the death of
Henry II. of France, July, 1559, but by this time the restored images
had again been removed. One day, when she came to St. Paul's, Dean
Nowell placed in her pew a prayer-book richly illuminated with German
scriptural engravings. She was very angry, and demanded to know
who had placed "this idolatrous book" on her cushion. The poor
Dean explained, and her Majesty was satisfied, but "prayed God to
give him more wisdom for the future." She expressed her satisfaction
that the pictures were German and not English. Some years later the
same Dean offended her in the opposite direction. It was on Ash
Wednesday, 1572; he was preaching before her, and denounced
certain "Popish superstitions," among them the use of the sign of

the Cross. Her Majesty called out to him sternly to "stick to his text." The next day he sent her a humble apology.

Paul's Cross was silent for some months; when at length it was again occupied the Reformed faith was reasserted. Bonner was sent to the Tower, and the English Communion service was again in use. In the following August, the Queen's Commissioners held a Visitation in St. Paul's, at which all who refused to conform with it were pronounced contumacious and deprived. The rood was again turned out, as were the images, and now it was with the approval of the people at large. In many places there was much violence displayed in the destruction, but not in St. Paul's. All was done there without tumult, and with discrimination. On December 17th, 1559, Parker was consecrated Archbishop at Lambeth, and four days later he consecrated Grindal Bishop of London. Bonner was sent to the Marshalsea Prison, which Strype declares was done to screen him from the popular detestation. He was well fed and housed there, and had "much enjoyment of his garden and orchards," until his death in 1569.

Grindal had been warmly attached to Ridley, and still loved his memory dearly. Moreover, he had himself been an exile for his opinions. He was not, therefore, likely to look favourably upon the old ceremonial, even in its modified form of stately solemnity and grace, such as Tallis and Merbecke would have preserved to it. And his Dean, Nowell, had the same distrust. Had they favoured it, in all probability the moderate and beautiful rendering of the Liturgy, as it is heard in the cathedral in our day, would not only have won the affections of the people at large, but would have arrested the strong tide o Puritanism and iconoclasm which was now rising. In Convocation, the Puritans nearly carried the removal of all organs from churches. They lost it by a majority of one, and Dean Nowell was in the minority.

Whilst the controversy was at its fiercest, on the 3rd of June, 1561, a violent thunderstorm burst over London. The Church of St. Martin's, Ludgate, was struck by lightning, and great masses of stones came down upon the pavement. Whilst people were looking dismayed at this, the steeple of St. Paul's was discovered to be on fire. The

E

timber framework had got ablaze, the lead which covered it poured down like lava upon the roof, the very bells melted. For four hours the whole cathedral was in danger, but happily, with the exception of the roof of the nave, the church was saved. As soon as the flames were extinguished, Pilkington, whose works are published by the Parker Society, furiously declared that it was all owing to the retention of Popery, and the other side, with equal vigour, attributed the disaster to the desecration by the Puritans.*

The steeple was never rebuilt, but the nave roof was begun without loss of time. Queen Elizabeth sent letters to the Lord Mayor, commanding him to take immediate steps, gave him 1000 marks from her own purse, and warrants for 1000 loads of timber from her woods. £7000 were raised at once by the clergy and laymen of London, "very frankly, lovingly, and willingly," says the Guildhall record. Before a month had elapsed a temporary roof was made, and in five years the lead roof was complete.

The victory over the Armada, in 1588, sent all England wild with delight. The Queen came in State to offer thanks at St. Paul's, attended by all the nobility, and after the sermon dined with the Bishop in his palace.

But the signs of irreverence and neglect are continually before us. We have already given extracts from sermons denouncing it. It was now that the raising of money by Government lotteries began, for the purpose of repairing the harbours, and a great shed was set up at the west door of St. Paul's for the drawing (1569). In 1605, four of the Gunpowder conspirators were hanged in front of the west door, and in the following May, Garnet, the Jesuit priest, shared the same fate on the same spot.

Let us before closing this chapter take note of the monuments of four Deans not mentioned in our last survey. They are Thomas Wynterbourne (Dean 1471-1478), William Worsley (1479-1499), a fine brass. William May we have already spoken of, Dean under Edward VI., deprived by Mary, restored by Elizabeth, elected Archbishop of York, but died the same day, August 8th, 1560. There were twelve Latin lines on his grave. His successor, Alexander Nowell,

---

* Milman's *Annals of St. Paul's*, pp. 280-1.

on a somewhat different historical footing from the Dean of St. Paul's, and it becomes necessary to say something about the latter.

The word Dean belongs to the ancient Roman law, *Decanus*, lit. one who has authority over ten, as a centurion was one who had authority over a hundred. The Deans seem originally to have been especially concerned with the management of funerals. Presently the name became adopted to Christian use, and was applied in monasteries to those who had charge of the discipline of every ten monks. When the Abbot was absent the senior Dean undertook the government; and thus it was that in cathedral churches which were monastic it gradually became the custom to have one who acted as Dean, and this system was gradually adopted in secular cathedrals, like St. Paul's. In monasteries, however, the Dean was so far subordinate to the Prior that he had charge of the music and ritual, while the Prior had a general superintendence.

The clergy of St. Paul's then were seculars. There were thirty of them, called Canons, as being entered on the list (καυών) of ecclesiastics serving the church. Each man was entitled to a portion of the income of the cathedral, and therefore was a " Prebendary," the name being derived from the daily rations (*præbenda*) served out to soldiers. There were thirty Canons or Prebendaries attached to St. Paul's, and these with the Bishop and Dean formed the Great Chapter. To them in theory belonged the right of electing the Bishop; but it was only theory, as it is still. The real nominator was the Pope or the King, whichever happened at the crisis to be in the ascendant.

In early days the Bishop was the ruling power inside the cathedral. At its first foundation, as we have seen, it was the Bishops who exerted themselves to raise the money for the building. But as time went on the Bishops, finding their hands full of affairs of state, stood aside in great measure, retired to their pleasant home at Fulham, and left to the Dean greater power. And thus it was that, as we have already told, Dean Ralph de Diceto built the Deanery. And thus gradually the Dean became practical ruler of the cathedral—the Bishop had no voice in affairs of the Chapter, except on appeal. And it is a curious fact that the Canons attempted to exclude the Dean from the managing body, as having no Prebend. He could expel from the choir, and punish the contumacious, but they contended that he had no power to touch the revenues. It was because of this that Bishop Sudbury (1370), in order to prevent the scandal of the Dean being excluded when the Chapter were discussing business, attached a prebendal stall to the Deanery, and thereby enabled him to preside, without possibility of cavil, at all meetings of the Chapter.

As the Canons, or at any rate many of them, had other churches, they had each his deputy, who said the service in the Cathedral. Each Prebendary had his own manor, and there were other manors which belonged to the common stock, and supplied the means of carrying on the services and paying the humbler officials. The Canons, it will be remembered, were secular, not monks; but they had a common "College," with a refectory, kitchen, brewhouse, bakehouse, and mill. Archdeacon Hale computed that the manors comprised in all about 24,000 acres, three-eighths of which were managed by the cathedral body, and the rest let to tenants, who had protecting rights of their own. In addition to these were the estates attached to the Deanery.

But with the changes which Time is always bringing, it came to pass that some of the Canons, who held other benefices (and the number increased as the years went on), preferred to live on their prebendal manors, or in their parishes; to follow, in short, the Bishop's example of non-attendance at the cathedral. And thus the services devolved on a few men who stayed on and were styled Residentiaries. These clerics not only had their keep at the common College, which increased in comfort and luxury, but also came in for large incomes from oblations, obits, and other privileges. At first it seemed irksome to be tied down to residence, but as time went on this became a privilege eagerly sought after; and thus grew up, what continues still, a chapter within the chapter, and the management of the cathedral fell into the hands of the Residentiaries.

The Treasurer was a canon of very great importance; the tithes of four churches came to him. He was entrusted with the duty of providing the lighting of the cathedral, and had charge of the relics, the books, the sacred vessels, crosses, curtains, and palls. The Sacrist had to superintend the tolling of the bells, to see that the church was opened at the appointed times, that it was kept clean, and that

A PONTIFICAL MASS. 'Ad te levavi animam meam.'
From a Missal of the Fifteenth Century. British Museum, 19897.

reverence was maintained at times of service. Under him were four Vergers (wand-bearers), who enforced the Sacrist's rules, and took care that bad characters were not harboured in the church, and that burden-bearers were kept out. We have seen that these duties fell largely into abeyance at certain times. Every Michaelmas Day the Verger appeared before the Dean to give up his wand, and to receive it back if his character was satisfactory. The Verger was bound to be a bachelor, because, said the statute, "having a wife is a troublesome and disturbing affair, and husbands are apt to study the wishes of their wives or their mistresses, and no man can serve two masters."

The Chancellor kept charge of the correspondence of the Chapter, and also superintended the schools belonging to the cathedral.

The Archdeacons of London, Middlesex, and Colchester had their own stalls in the cathedral, but had no voice in the Chapter.

The Minor Canons, twelve in number, formed a separate college, founded in the time of Richard II. They were, of course, under the authority of the cathedral, though they had independent estates of their own.

The Scriptorium of St. Paul's was an important department, and was well managed   Much of the work produced in it perished in the fire; but there are some of its manuscripts still happily preserved, notably the *Majora Statuta* of the cathedral, in the Library there, and a magnificent folio of Diceto's History, now in Lambeth .Library.

Incidental notice has been taken in the preceding pages of Chantries in St. Paul's, but we have to speak more fully of these, for they formed a very large source of income, especially to the Residentiary Canons. These Chantries were founded for saying masses for the souls of the departed, even to the end of the world. St. Paul's was almost beyond measure rich in them. The oldest was founded in the reign of Henry II., after which time they multiplied so fast that it would be impossible to enumerate them all here. There is a return of them (quoted at length by Dugdale), which was made by order of King Edward VI. Take the description of the second of them as he gives it. " The next was ordained by Richard, surnamed Nigell [Fitzneal], Bishop of London in King Richard I.'s time, who having built two altars in this cathedral, the one dedicated to St. Thomas the

Martyr, and the other to St. Dionis, assigned eight marks yearly rent, to be received out of the church of Cestreheart, for the maintaining of two priests celebrating every day thereat; viz., one for the good estate of the King of England and Bishop of London for the time being; as also for all the congregation of this church, and the faithful parishioners belonging thereto, and the other for the souls of the Kings of England and Bishops of London, and all the faithful deceased : which grant was confirmed by the Chapter." This is a fair specimen; they go on page after page in Dugdale's folio. William de Sanctæ Mariæ ecclesia (he was Dean 1241-1243) leaves 120 marks for bread and beer yearly to a priest who shall celebrate for his soul and for the souls of his predecessors, successors, parents, and benefactors. Sometimes special altars are named at which the Mass is to be said, "St. Chad, St. Nicholas, St. Ethelbert the King, St. Radegund, St. James, the twelve Apostles, St. John the Evangelist, St. John Baptist, St. Erkenwald, St. Sylvester, St. Michael, St. Katharine." I take them as they come in the successive testaments. The following passage is worth quoting :—" In 19 Ed. II. Roger de Waltham, a Canon of this church, enfeoft the Dean and Chapter of certain messuages and shops lying within the city of London, for the support of two priests to pray perpetually for his soul, and for the souls of his parents and benefactors, within the chapel of St. John the Baptist in the south part of this cathedral ; as also for the soul of Antony Beck, Patriarch of Jerusalem, and Bishop of Durham. And further directed that out of the revenue of these messuages, &c., there should be a yearly allowance to the said Dean and Chapter, to keep solemn processions in this church on the several days of the invention and exaltation of the Holy Cross, as also of St. John Baptist ; wearing their copes at those times in such sort as they used on all the great festivals ; and likewise out of his high devotion to the service of God, and that it should be the more venerably performed therein, he gave divers costly vestments thereto, some whereof were set with precious stones, expressly directing that in all masses wherein himself by particular name was to be commended, as also at his anniversary, and in those festivals of the Holy Cross, St. John Baptist, and St. Laurence the Deacon, they should be used. And, moreover, out of his abundant piety he founded a certain Oratory on the south side of the Choir in this

JOHN FISHER, BISHOP OF ROCHESTER. *After Holbein.*

ST. MATTHEW. *View of a Mediæval Scriptorium.*
From a MS. of a Book of Prayers. 15th Century.
British Museum, Slo. 2468.

A REQUIEM MASS.
From a MS. of a Book of Prayers, 15th Century.
British Museum, Slo. 2468.

SINGING THE PLACEBO.
From a MS. of Hours of the Virgin, &c. Fifteenth Century.
British Museum, Harl. 2971.

SEALS OF THE DEAN AND CHAPTER.
From Casts in the Library of St. Paul's Cathedral.

ORGAN AND TRUMPETS.

From a Collection of Miniatures from Choral Service Books. Fourteenth Century.
British Museum, 29902.

cathedral, towards the upper end thereof, to the honour of God, our Lady, St. Laurence, and All Saints, and adorned it with the images of our blessed Saviour, St. John Baptist, St. Laurence, and St. Mary Magdalene ; so likewise with the pictures of the celestial Hierarchy, the joys of the blessed Virgin, and others, both in the roof about the altar, and other places within and without ; in which Oratory the chantry before mentioned was placed, and the said anniversary to be kept. And, lastly, in the south wall, opposite to the said Oratory, erected a glorious tabernacle, which contained the image of the said blessed Virgin, sitting as it were in childbed ; as also of our Saviour, in swaddling clothes, lying between the ox and the ass, and St. Joseph at her feet ; above which was another image of her, standing with the child in her arms. And on the beam, thwarting from the upper end of the Oratory to the before-specified childbed, placed the crowned images of our Saviour and his mother sitting in one tabernacle ; as also the images of St. Katharine and St. Margaret, virgins and martyrs ; neither was there any part of the said Oratory, or roof thereof, but he caused it to be beautified with comely pictures and images, to the end that the memory of our blessed Saviour and His saints, especially of the glorious Virgin, His mother, might be always the more famous: in which Oratory he designed that his sepulture should be."

Bishop Richard of Gravesend (d. at Fulham, 1306) made his will at his Manor House of Haringay, in 1302. It is written with his own hand, and the opening words are: "Imprimis, Tibi, o pie Redemptor, et potens Salvator animarum, Domine Jesu Christe, animam meam commendo ; Tibi etiam, o summe Sacerdos et vere Pontifex animarum, commendo universam plebem Londonensis civitatis et diocæsis; obsecrans te, per medicinam vulnerum tuorum, qui in cruce pependisti, ut mihi et ipsis, concessa perfecta venia peccatorum, concedas nos ad tuam misericordiam pervenire, et frui beatitudine, tuis electis perenniter repromissâ." After which he goes on to direct that he shall be buried close to his predecessor, Henry de Sandwiche, whom he calls his special benefactor, and that the marble covering his grave shall not rise higher than the pavement ; that out of his personal estate, consisting of books, household goods, corn and cattle, which together is valued at 2000 marks, 140*l.* shall be given to the poor, 100 marks to the new fabric of the cathedral, and that lands of the value of 10*l.* a year shall be bought for the founding of a chantry here for his soul, and for the keeping of his anniversary.

In the Inventory of his goods we have interesting information about values: wheat is reckoned at 4*s.* the quarter, peas at 2*s.* 6*d.*, and oats at 2*s.* Bulls are worth 7*s.* 4*d.* each, kine 6*s.*, fat muttons 1*s.*, ewes 8*d.*, capons 2*d.*, cocks and hens 1*d.* His nephew, Stephen, who succeeded him thirteen years later, allows only 100 marks for the expenses of his funeral, quoting St. Augustine that funeral parade may be a certain comfort to the living, but is of no advantage to the dead. He disposes of 140*l.* to the poor tenants on his manors. Bishop Michael Northburgh (d. 1362) left the rents of certain houses which he had built at Fulham for a chantry priest, who was to be appointed by the Bishop of London. He also desired to be buried on the same day he died, with his face exposed to view, outside the west door of the cathedral. His endowment of the chantry being judged to be insufficient, one of the nominated chantry priests gave a further endowment for it. This Bishop Northburgh left 2000*l.* for the completion of the house of the Carthusians (Charter House) in co-operation with Sir Walter Manny. He also left 1000 marks to be put into a chest in the Cathedral Treasury, out of which any poor layman might, for a sufficient pledge, borrow 10*l.*, the Dean and principal Canons 20*l.* upon the like pledge; the Bishop 40*l.*; other noblemen or citizens 20*l.* for the term of a year. If at the year's end the money was not repaid, the preacher at Paul's Cross was to notify the fact, and to announce that the pledge would be sold within fourteen days if it were not redeemed, and any surplus from the sale would be handed to the borrower, or his executors. If there were no executors then the money was to go back to the chest, and be spent for the health of his soul. There were three keys to the chest, one was kept by the Dean, another by the oldest Canon-resident, and the third by a Warden appointed by the Chapter.

One keeps on finding benefactions of this sort. In 1370 one John Hiltoft's executors handed over some money which the Chapter employed in repairing some ruined houses; but they took care to establish a chantry of one chaplain to celebrate Divine service daily in St. Dunstan's Chapel for the soul of the said John.

We have already made mention of the chantry which Henry IV. founded to the memory of his father and mother. Bishop Braybrooke on that occasion gave a piece of ground, part of his palace, 36 feet by 19 feet, for the habitation of the priests attached to this chantry. And King Henry, we are told, " gave to the Dean and Chapter, and their successors, for ever, divers messuages and lands, lying within the City of London, for the anniversary of the said John, Duke of Lancaster, his father, on the 4th day of February, and of Blanch, his mother, on the 12th day of September yearly in this church, with Placebo and Dirige, nine Antiphons, nine Psalms, and nine Lessons, in the exequies of either of them ; as also Mass of Requiem, with note, on the morrow to be performed at the high altar for ever ; and moreover to distribute unto the said Dean and Chapter these several sums, viz., to the Dean, as often as he shall be present, three shillings and fourpence ; to the principal canons, twenty pence (to the sum of 16s. 8d.) ; to the petty canons, ten shillings ; to the chaplains, twenty shillings ; to the vicars, four shillings and eightpence ; to the choristers, two shillings and sixpence ; to the vergers, twelvepence ; to the bell-ringers, fourpence ; to the keeper of the lamps about the tomb of the said duke and duchess, at each of their said anniversaries, sixpence ; to the Mayor of London for the time being, in respect of his presence at the said anniversaries, three shillings and fourpence ; to the Bishop of London, for the rent of the house where the said chantry priests did reside, ten shillings ; and for to find eight great tapers to burn about that tomb on the day of the said anniversaries, at the exequies, and mass on the morrow, and likewise at the processions, masses, and vespers on every great festival, and upon Sundays at the procession, mass, and second vespers for ever. And lastly, to provide for those priests belonging to that chapel on the north part of the said tomb, a certain chalice, missal, and portvoise [Breviary] according to the Ordinale Sarum ; as also vestments, bread, wine, wax, and glasses, and other ornaments and necessaries for the same, and repairs of their mansion." A few years later another chantry was founded at the same altar for the soul of Henry IV. himself.

As years went on, the provision for all these Chantries being found inadequate to maintain them, some were united together, and thus, at their dissolution in the first year of Edward VI., it was found that there were only thirty-five, to which belonged fifty-four priests.

In addition to the Chantries were the *Obits*, held by the Dean and Canons, particular anniversaries of deaths. They varied in value according to the donors' endowment from 4*l.* to 10*s.* Dugdale gives a long list of them.

This cathedral was wonderfully rich in plate and jewels, so much so that, as Dugdale says, the very inventory would fill a volume. To take only one illustration : King John of France when he was brought here by the Black Prince " gave an oblation of twelve nobles at the shrine of St. Erkenwald, the same at that of the Annunciation, twenty-six floren nobles at the Crucifix by the north door, four basins of gold at the high altar ; and, at the hearing of Mass, after the Offertory, gave to the Dean then officiating, five floren nobles, which the said Dean and John Lyllington (the weekly petty canon), his assistant, had. All which being performed, he gave, moreover, in the chapter-house, fifty floren nobles to be distributed amongst the officers of the church."

With regard to the character of the services before the Reformation, we have but few data to go upon. In 1414 Bishop Richard Clifford, with the consent of the Dean and Chapter, ordained that from the first day of December following, the use of Sarum should be observed. Up to that time there had been a special " Usus Sancti Pauli."

There was an organ in the church, or rather, to use the old phrase, a " pair of organs," for the instrument had a plural name like " a pair of bellows." Organs were in use in the church at any rate in the fourth century, and were introduced into England by Archbishop Theodore. In old times there was no official organist ; the duty was taken by the master of the choristers or one of the gentlemen of the choir. In churches of the regular foundation a monk played.

English Church music, in its proper sense, began with the Reformation. In the Roman Church, the great genius of Palestrina had produced nothing less than a revolution as regards the ancient Plain Song; and with the English Liturgy we associate the honoured names of Tallis, Merbecke, Byrd, Farrant in the early days, and a splendid list of successors right down to our time, wherein is still no falling off. Tallis is supposed by Rimbault to have been a pupil of

Mulliner, the organist of St. Paul's, but there is no evidence to support this. It must be confessed that his service in the Dorian mode, which heads the collection in Boyce's Cathedral Music, and which is indeed the first harmonised setting of the Canticles ever composed for the English Liturgy, is very dull, but his harmony of the Litany and of the Versicles after the Creed, has never been equalled for beauty. His Canon tune, to which we sing Ken's Evening Hymn, is also unsurpassed, and his anthem, "If ye love Me," is one of wonderful sweetness and devout feeling. John Redford was his contemporary, and was organist of St. Paul's, 1530–1540. His anthem, "Rejoice in the Lord," is as impressive and stately as Tallis's that I have just named. It is frequently sung at St. Paul's still. William Byrd was senior chorister of St. Paul's in 1554. I hold his service in D minor to be the finest which had as yet been set to the Reformed Liturgy—the Nicene Creed in particular is of marvellous beauty. Tallis had not attempted "expression" in his setting of the Canticles. The meaning seems to breathe all through Byrd's harmonies. I did not know until I read Sir George Grove's article upon him, that Byrd secretly remained a Roman Catholic, but I long ago made up my mind, on my own judgment, that his most pathetic anthem, "Bow thine ear," was a wail over the iconoclasm in St. Paul's. He died in extreme old age in 1623. Morley was another organist of St. Paul's, the author of a fine setting of the Burial Service. Paul Hentzner, who visited St. Paul's in 1598, says in his *Itinerary*, "It has a very fine organ, which at evensong, accompanied with other instruments, makes excellent music."

Concerning the dramatic performances which went on in the cathedral at certain times, there is nothing peculiar to St. Paul's that I know of to mention. These performances were originally intended for instruction, pictorial representations of scenes from the Bible and Church History, but often degenerating into coarse buffoonery and horseplay. The "Boy Bishop" was for many generations an established institution. One ceremony there was, peculiar to St. Paul's, namely, "The Offering of a Buck and Doe." Sir William le Baud in 1328 made a yearly grant to the Dean and Canons of a doe to be presented on the Feast of the Conversion of St. Paul, and of a fat buck to be offered at the midsummer commemoration of the same Apostle.

BISHOP AND CANONS IN THE CHURCH OF ST. GREGORY-BY-ST. PAUL.

In purpose fully, yiff it wolde be,
To karye the martir fro thenys prevyly.
But whan the bysshop was therto most besy
With the body to Poulis forto gon,
Yt stood as fyx as a gret hill off ston.

Multitude ther myhte noon avayle,
Al be they dyde ther fforce and besy peyne ;
For but in ydel they spent ther travayle.
The peple lefte, the bysshop gan dysdeyne :
Drauht off corde nor off no myhty chayne
Halp lyte or nouht—this myracle is no fable—
For lik a mount it stood ylyche stable.

Wherupon the bysshop gan mervaylle,
Fully diffraudyd off his entencion.
And whan ther power and fforce gan to faylle,
Ayllewyn kam neer with humble affeccion,
Meekly knelyng sayde his orysoun :
The kyng requeryng lowly for Crystes sake
His owyn contre he sholde not forsake.

With this praier Ayllewyn aroos,
Gan ley to hand : fond no resistence,
Took the chest wher the kyng lay cloos,
Leffte hym up withoute violence.
The bysshop thanne with dreed and reverence
Conveyed hym forth with processioun,
Till he was passid the subarbis off the toun.

Inter Chorum et alam australem.

MONUMENT OF DR. DONNE. *After W. Hollar.*

PREACHING AT PAUL'S CROSS BEFORE JAMES I. *From a painting by H. Farley.*
Collection of the Society of Antiquaries.

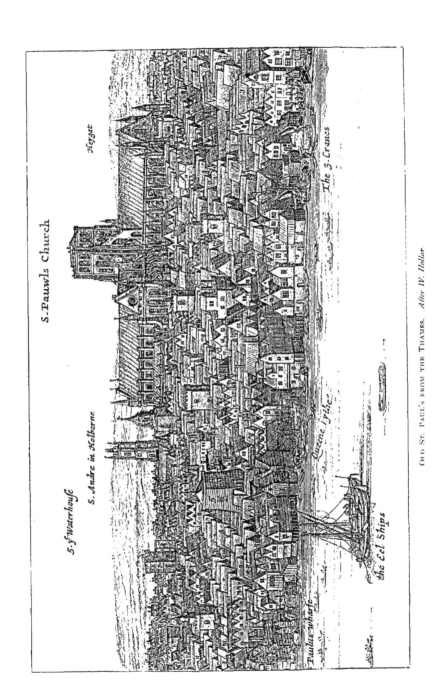

OLD ST. PAUL'S FROM THE THAMES. *After W. Hollar.*

WEST FRONT AFTER THE FIRE. *From a drawing in the Library of St. Paul's Cathedral.*

He now took the lead in the restoration of St. Paul's. It must be acknowledged that after the first outburst of zeal following the fire of 1561, St. Paul's was much neglected for many long years. The authorities were lukewarm, the services were dead and unattractive, and all manner of irreverence was seen there daily. Bishop Earle's *Microcosmography* (1628) often gets quoted, but his description of " Paule's Walke " ought to find place here. I take it from a contemporary MS. copy. Paul's Walk was the whole nave of the cathedral :—" Paule's Walke is the lande's epitomy, or you may call it, the lesser Ile [Aisle] of Greate Brittayne. It is more than this, the whole woorlde's map, which you may here discerne in its perfect motion, justling and turning. It is an heape of stones and men, with a vast confusion of languages, and were the steeple not sanctified, nothing liker Babell. The noyse of it is like that of bees, an humming buzze mixed with walking tongues, and feet. It is a kind of still rore, or loude whisper. It is the greate exchange of all discourse, and noe business whatsoever but it is here stirring and on foote. It is the Synode of all pates politicke, jointed and layed together in most serious postures ; and they are not halfe soe busy at the Parliament. It is the anticke of tayles to tayles, and backes to backes, and for vizzards you neede goe noe further than faces. Tis the market of young lecturers, which you may cheapen at all rates and sizes. It is the generall mint of famous lyes, which are here (like the legendes of Popery) first coyned, and stamped in the church. All inventions are emptied here, and not few pockettes. The best signe of a temple in it, is that it is the thieves' sanctuary, whoe rob here more safely in a crowde than in a wildernesse, whilst every searcher is a bush to hide them in. It is the other expence of a day after playes and the taverne . . . . and men have still some othes left to swear here. . . . . The visitants are all men without exception, but the principall inhabitants are stale knights and captains out of servis, men with long rapiers and breeches, who after all turne merchant here, and trafficke for news. Some make it a preface to dinner and travell for a stomache, but thriftier men make it their ordinary, and boarde here very cheape. Of all such places it is least troubled with hobgoblins, for if a ghost would walk here he could not." Of "the singing men" he draws a most unfavourable picture, accuses them of drunkenness and

F

shameful looseness of life; says that they are earnest in evil deeds and that their work in the cathedral is their recreation. Bishop Pilkington also speaks of the profanity and worldliness of the daily frequenters. The carrying merchandise into the building seems to have been the custom in many of the cathedrals, and so it is not wonderful that the building went to ruin. The Bishop of London, Laud, sent round exhortations to the City Companies to contribute to the restoration. Here is his letter to the Barber Surgeons, dated January 30th, 1632 :—

"To the right worshipful my very worthy friends the Master Wardens and Assistants of the Company of Barber Surgeons, London, these :

"*Salus in Christo.* After my very hearty commendations you cannot but take notice of his Majesty's most honest and pious intention for the repair of the decay of Saint Paul's Church here in London, being the mother church of this City and Diocese, and the great Cathedral of this Kingdom. A great dishonour it is, not only to this City, but to the whole state to see that ancient and goodly pile of building so decayed as it is, but it will be a far greater if care should not be taken to prevent the fall of it into ruin. And it would be no less disgrace to religion, happily established in this kingdom, if it should have so little power over the minds of men as not to prevail with them to keep those eminent places of God's service in due and decent repair, which their forefathers built in times, by their own confession, not so full of the knowledge of God's truth as this present age is. I am not ignorant how many worthy works have been done of late in and about this City towards the building and repairing of churches, which makes me hope that every man's purse will open to this great and necessary work (according to God's blessing upon him), so much tending to the service of God and the honour of this nation. The general body of this City have done very worthily in their bounty already, also the Lord Mayor, Aldermen and Sheriffs severally, for their own persons. These are, therefore, according to their examples, heartily to pray and desire you, the Master Warden and other assistants of the worthy Company of Barber Surgeons to contribute out of your public stock to the work aforesaid, what you out of your charity and devotion shall think fit, and to pay the sum resolved on by you into the Chamber of London at or before our Lady Day next, praying you that I may receive by any servant of your Company a note what the sum is which you resolve to give. And for this charity of yours, whatever it shall prove to be, I shall not only give you hearty thanks, but be as ready to serve you, and every of you, as you are to serve God and His Church. So, not doubting of your love and forwarding to this great work, I leave you to the grace of God, and shall so rest,   " Your very loving Friend,

                                  " GUL : LONDON."

The Court considered this letter on the 9th of April following, and agreed to pay £10 down, and the same sum each year for the next nine years.

We must not omit one munificent donor who came forward now : Sir Paul Pindar, who had made a large fortune as a Turkey merchant, and had been sent by King James as Ambassador to Constantinople, gave over £10,000 to the restoration of the cathedral. He died in 1650, and his beautifully picturesque house remained in Bishopsgate Street (it had been turned, like Crosby Hall, into a tavern) until 1890, when it was pulled down. Some of the most striking portions of its architecture are preserved in the Kensington Museum.

That the alterations and additions of Inigo Jones, under King James, were altogether incongruous with the old building everybody will admit. But there are excuses to be made. He knew very little about Gothic architecture. The only example now remaining of his attempts in this style is the Chapel of Lincoln's Inn. St. Katharine Cree in the City has been attributed to him, but with little probability. And if he had essayed to work in Gothic at St. Paul's, it would not have been in accordance with precedent. Nearly all our great cathedrals display endless varieties of style, because it was the universal practice of our forefathers to work in the style current in their own time. We rejoice to see Norman and Perpendicular under one roof, though they represent periods 400 years apart. In the case before us Gothic architecture had died out for the time being. Not only our Reformers, who did not require aisles for processions nor rich choirs, but the Jesuits also, who had sprung suddenly into mighty power on the Continent, repudiated mediæval art, and strove to adapt the classical reaction in Europe to their own tenets. Nearly all the Jesuit churches abroad are classical.

It was, no doubt, fortunate that Inigo Jones confined his work at St. Paul's to some very poor additions to the transepts, and to a portico, very magnificent in its way, at the west end. He would have destroyed, doubtless, much of the noble nave in time; but his work was abruptly brought to an end by the outbreak of the Civil War. The work had languished for some years, under the continuance of causes which I have already adduced. But Laud, as Bishop of London, had displayed most praiseworthy zeal, and King Charles had supported him generously. When the troubles began, the funds ceased. In 1640 there had been contributions amounting to £10,000. In 1641 they fell to less than £2000; in 1643 to £15. In 1642 Paul's Cross had been pulled down, and in the following March Parliament seized on the revenues of the cathedral.

With the Rebellion the history of the cathedral may be said to be a blank. It would have been troublesome and expensive to pull it down, so it was left to decay; the revenues were seized for military uses, and the sacred vessels sold. There is a doubtful tradition that Cromwell tried to sell the building to the Jews for a stately synagogue. Inigo Jones's portico was let out for shops, the nave was turned into cavalry barracks. An order, quoted by Sir Henry Ellis, of which there is a copy in the British Museum, came out in 1651 prohibiting the soldiers from playing at ninepins from nine p.m. till six a.m., as the noise disturbs the residents in the neighbourhood, and they are also forbidden to disturb the peaceable passers by. At the Church of St. Gregory by St. Paul, towards the latter part of Cromwell's life, it is said that the liturgy of the Church was regularly used, through the influence of his daughter, Elizabeth Claypole, and not only so, but that he used sometimes to attend it under the same auspices.

Once more before the catastrophe let us pause and see what monuments had been erected in the Cathedral since the Stuarts mounted the throne. Dean VALENTINE CAREY was also Bishop of Exeter, d. 1626, a High Churchman. He "imprudently commended the soul of a dead person to the mercies of God, which he was forced to retract." There was a brass to him with mitre and his arms, but no figure.

Then we come to a monument which has a very great and unique interest, that of Dr. John Donne, who was Dean from 1621 to 1631. It is hardly needful to say that his life is the first in the beautiful set of biographies by his friend, Izaak Walton. But it seems only right to quote Walton's account of this monument. The Dean knew that he was dying, and his friends expressed their desire to know his wishes. He sent for a carver to make for him in wood the figure of an urn, giving him directions for the compass and height of it, and to bring with it a board, of the just height of his body. " These being got, then without delay a choice painter was got to be in readiness to draw his picture, which was taken as followeth :—Several charcoal fires being first made in his large study, he brought with him into that place his winding-sheet in his hand, and, having put off all his clothes, had this sheet put on him, and so tied with knots at his head and feet, and his hands so placed as dead bodies are usually fitted to be shrouded and put into their coffin or grave. Upon this urn he thus stood, with his eyes shut, and with so much of the sheet turned aside as might show his lean, pale, and death-like face, which was purposely turned towards the East, from whence he expected the second coming of his and our Saviour Jesus." In this posture he was drawn at his just height ; and when the picture was fully finished, he caused it to be set by his bedside, where it continued, and became his hourly object till his death, and was then given to his dearest friend and executor, Dr. Henry King, then chief Residentiary of St. Paul's, who caused him to be thus carved in one entire piece of white marble, as it now stands in that church ; and, by Dr. Donne's own appointment, these words were affixed to it as an epitaph :—

JOHANNES DONNE
Sac. Theol. Profess.
Post varia studia, quibus ab annis
Tenerrimis fideliter, nec infeliciter
incubuit ;
Instinctu et impulsu Spiritus Sancti, monitu
et hortatu
Regis Jacobi, ordines sacros amplexus
Anno sui Jesu, MDCXIV. et suæ ætatis XLII.
Decanatu hujus ecclesiæ indutus,
XXVII. Novembris, MDCXXI.
Exutus morte ultimo die Martii MDCXXXI.
Hic, licet in occiduo cinere, aspicit eum
Cujus nomen est oriens.

house which that King had given him at Blackfriars, December 9th, 1641, and was buried close by John of Gaunt.

We must not omit mention of John Tomkins, Organist of the Cathedral. He died in 1638. His epitaph says that he was the most celebrated organist of his time. He succeeded Orlando Gibbons at King's College, Cambridge, in 1606, and came to St. Paul's in 1619. His compositions, though good, are not numerous, but he is said to have been a wonderful executant.

But we must now approach the final scenes of Old St. Paul's. At the Restoration, Sheldon was made Bishop of London, and two years later, on his translation to Canterbury, was succeeded by Humphrey Henchman, a highly respectable man, who owed his elevation to his loyalty to the Stuarts during the Commonwealth. He took no part in public affairs, but was a liberal contributor to the funds of the cathedral. The Dean, John Barwick, was a good musician, and restored the choir of the cathedral to decent and orderly condition. But it was soon found that the building was in an insecure, indeed dangerous condition, and it became a pressing duty to put it in safe order. Inigo Jones had died in 1652, and the Dean, Sancroft, who had succeeded Barwick in 1664, called on Dr. Christopher Wren to survey the cathedral and report upon it.

This famous man was the son of the Rector of East Knoyle, in Wilts, and was born in 1632. His father had some skill in architecture, for he put a new roof to his church, and he taught his son to draw, an art in which he displayed extraordinary skill and taste. He was sent to Westminster School, and, under the famous Busby, became a good scholar. Then he went to Wadham College, Oxford, the Master of which, Wilkins, afterwards Bishop of Chester, was a great master of science. Wren took advantage of his opportunities, and became so well known for his acquirements in mathematics and his successful experiments in natural science that he was elected to a Fellowship at All Souls'. A few years later he was appointed to the Professorship of Astronomy at Gresham College, and his brilliant reputation made his rooms a meeting-place of the men who subsequently founded the Royal Society. A fresh preferment, that to the Chair of Savilian Professor of Astronomy at Oxford, did not hinder him from pursuing a fresh line. His father, as we have said, taught him to draw, his mathematical skill guided his judgment in construction, and these two acquirements turned him more and more towards architecture, though even now he was held second only to Newton as a philosopher. His first appearance as an architect was his acceptance of the post of Surveyor of King Charles II.'s public works. This was in 1661. He lost no time in starting in his new profession, for in 1663 he designed the chapel of Pembroke College, Cambridge, which his uncle Matthew gave, and the Sheldonian Theatre at Oxford. This, then, brings him down to the survey of St. Paul's above named. It was carefully made, and presented in May, 1666. How he designed to rebuild some portions which were decayed, to introduce more light, to cut off the corners of the cross and erect a central dome—all this boots not now to tell. The plans were drawn, and estimates were ordered on Monday, August 27th, 1666.

But before another week had passed an effectual end was put for many a day to all plans for the "repair of the cathedral." Pepys begins his diary of September 2nd with the following words :—
"Lord's Day.—Some of our maids sitting up late last night to get things ready against our feast to-day, Jane calls us up about three in the morning to tell us of a great fire they saw in the City ; so I rose and slipped on my night-gown and went to her window, and thought it to be on the back of Mark Lane at the farthest." He thought this was far enough off and went to bed again. But next day he realises that it is all a terrible business, and so he goes on to tell how he walked about the streets and in some places burned his shoes ; went on the river, where the hot fiery flakes pursued him ; went to the King and gave advice and received instructions ; met the Lord Mayor who seemed out of his senses. So he goes on with his well-known description until September 7th, when he was " Up by five o'clock, and blessed be God! find all well, and by water to Paul's Wharf. Walked thence and saw all the town burned, and a miserable sight of Paul's Church, with all the roof fallen, and the body of the choir fallen into St. Faith's; Paul's School also, Ludgate, and Fleet Street."

Evelyn's note of the disaster is written in a higher key. "September 3rd . . . . I went and saw the whole south part of the City burning from Cheapeside to the Thames, and all along Cornehill (for it likewise kindl'd back against the wind as well as forward), Tower Streete, Fen-church Streete, Gracious Streete, and so along to Bainard's Castle, and was now taking hold of St. Paule's Church, to which the scaffolds contributed exceedingly. The conflagration was so universal, and the people so astonish'd, that from the beginning, I know not by what despondency or fate, they hardly stirr'd to quench it, so that there was nothing heard or seene but crying out and lamentation, running about like distracted creatures, without at all attempting to save even their goods — such a strange consternation there was upon them, so as it burned both in breadth and length, the churches, public halls, Exchange, hospitals, monuments, and ornaments, leaping after a prodigious manner from house to house and streete to streete, at greate distances one from the other ; for the heate, with a long set of faire and warme weather, had even ignited the aire and prepar'd the materials to conceive the fire, which devour'd after an incredible manner, houses, furniture, and everything. Here we saw the Thames cover'd with goods floating, all the barges and boates laden with what some had time and courage to save, as, on the other, the carts, &c., carrying out to the fields, which for many miles were strew'd with moveables of all sorts, and tents erecting to shelter both people and what goods they could get away. Oh, the miserable and calamitous spectacle, such as haply the world had not seene the like since the foundation of it, nor be outdone till the universal conflagration of it. All the skie was of a fiery aspect, like the top of a burning oven, and the light seene above forty miles round about for many nights. God grant mine eyes may never behold the like, who now saw above 10,000 houses all in one flame ; the noise and crackling and thunder of the impetuous flames, the shreiking of women and children, the hurry of people, the fall of Towers, Houses, and Churches, was like an hideous storme, and the aire all about so hot and inflam'd that, at the last, one was not able to approach it, so that they were forc'd to stand still and let the flames burn on, which they did for neere two miles in length and one in bredth. The clowds also of smoke were dismall, and reach'd, upon computation, neer fifty-six miles in length. Thus I left it this afternoone burning, a resemblance of Sodom or the last day. It forcibly call'd to my mind that passage—*non enim hic habemus stabilem civitatem*: the ruines resembling the picture of Troy—London was, but is no more! Thus I returned home.

"September 7th.—I went this morning on foote from White-hall as far as London Bridge, thro' the late Fleete-streete, Ludgate Hill, by St. Paules, Cheapeside, Exchange, Bishopsgate, Aldersgate, and on to Moorefields, thence thro' Cornehill, &c., with extraordinary difficulty, clambering over heaps of yet smoking rubbish, and frequently mistaking where I was . . . .

"At my returne I was infinitely concern'd to find that goodly Church St. Paules now a sad ruine, and that beautifull portico (for structure comparable to any in Europe, as not long before repair'd by the late King) now rent in pieces, flakes of vast stone split asunder, and nothing now remaining intire but the inscription in the architrave, shewing by whom it was built, which had not one letter of it defac'd. It was astonishing to see what immense stones the heate had in a manner calcin'd, so that all the ornaments, columns, freezes, capitals, and pro-jectures of massie Portland-stone flew off, even to the very roofe, where a sheet of lead covering a great space (no less than six akers by measure) was totally mealted ; the ruines of the vaulted roofe falling broke into St. Faith's, which being fill'd with the magazines of bookes belonging to the Stationers, and carried thither for safety, they were all consum'd, burning for a weeke following. It is also observable that the lead over the altar at the East end was untouch'd, and among the divers monuments, the body of one Bishop remain'd intire. Thus lay in ashes that most venerable Church, one of the most antient pieces of early piety in the Christian world."

Sancroft, who was Dean at the time of the fire, and who afterwards became Archbishop, was anxious to restore the cathedral on the old lines. Henchman was Bishop, but he left the matter for the Dean to deal with, though he not only rebuilt the Bishop's Palace at his own expense but contributed munificently to the new building. Sancroft preached within the ruined building before the King on October 10th, 1667, from the text, "His compassions fail not," and the sermon is really eloquent. The congregation was gathered at the west end, which had been hastily fitted up. The east end was absolute ruin.

Wren had already declared that it was impossible to restore the old building, and in the following April, Sancroft wrote to him that he had been right in so judging. "Our work at the west end," he wrote, "has fallen about our ears." Two pillars had come down with a crash, and the rest was so unsafe that men were afraid to go near, even to pull it down. He added, "You are so absolutely necessary to us that we can do nothing, resolve on nothing without you." This settled the question.

There is a little difficulty with regard to the drawing, preserved in the library of the cathedral, of the West Front after the Fire. Evelyn, as we have seen, seems to describe it as far more ruinous than the picture before us shows. Perhaps the artist filled up some of the details from his memory, for the drawing hardly looks so desolate a ruin as Evelyn implies. The gable of the nave roof is striking enough, and evidently exactly according to fact; and the tower of St. Gregory's preserves its external form, though it is inwardly consumed, as is the whole nave. I am inclined to judge that this is substantially the appearance of the porch after the west end had been fitted up for worship as Sancroft described. However, Wren had condemned the structure as unsafe, and the Dean had acquiesced, and the new cathedral was resolved upon.

There was delay, which was inevitable. Not only was the whole city paralysed with the awful extent of the ruin, but there were questions which had to be referred to Parliament, as to the method of raising the funds. Happily the whole voice of the people was of one accord in recognising that it was a paramount duty for the nation to build a splendid cathedral, worthy of England and of her capital city. It was not until November 1673 that the announcement was made of the determination of the King and his Parliament to rebuild St. Paul's. The history of that rebuilding belongs to New St. Paul's. The King wanted to employ a French architect, Claude Perrault, who had built the new front of the Louvre, but this was objected to. Then Denham, whose life may be read in Johnson's Poets, and who wrote one poem which may still be met with, *Cooper's Hill*, was appointed the King's Surveyor, with Wren for his "Coadjutor." Denham held the title to his death, but had nothing to do with the work. He died next year, and Wren then held unquestioned possession. His account of the old building, the principal features of which have been borrowed in the foregoing paper, is given in his son's book entitled *Parentalia*. Our plan shows a change which Wren made as to the orientation. In all probability this arose out of his scrupulous care as to the nature of the foundation. The clearing away was most difficult. Parts had to be blown up with gunpowder. It is said that when he was giving instructions to the builders on clearing away the ruins, he called on a workman to bring a great flat stone, which he might use as a centre in marking out on the ground the circle of the dome. The man took out of the rubbish the first large stone that came to hand, which was a piece of gravestone, and, when it was laid down, it was found to have on it the single word "RESURGAM." He took this, and there was no superstition in such an idea, as a promise from God.

INDEX

Milton Keynes UK
Ingram Content Group UK Ltd.
UKHW022026110124
435898UK00005B/97